HEALING
DAY *by* DAY

—⚬—

Scripture, reflections, practices, and prayers

MARCI ALBORGHETTI

TWENTY
THIRD 23rd
PUBLICATIONS
www.23rdpublications.com

Twenty-Third Publications

1 Montauk Avenue, Suite 200, New London, CT 06320

(860) 437-3012 » (800) 321-0411 » www.23rdpublications.com

Cover photo: ©iStockphoto.com/andDraw

ISBN: 978-1-62785-000-1

Library of Congress Catalog Card Number: 2014935254

Printed in the U.S.A.

Introduction

I spent the first thirty-five years of my life relatively complacent about healing. Granted, I'd had the occasional flu or stomach bug, a few aches and pains, and even breaks and strains. But when a doctor told me when I was thirty-six that if he hadn't found and removed an in situ melanoma from the center of my back, it could have developed into a fatal cancer, I found my interest in healing telescoping rather swiftly. When he added that I'd likely be living with this shadow all my life, it was all I could do not to panic.

We are all in need of healing. It is in our human nature to be broken, hurt, fragile, ill. It is this need for healing that reminds us always of our need for God. Our fragility is a constant echo of Saint Paul's claim that it is our weakness that allows God's strength to shine through. There are so many human conditions that require God's healing. From allergies to lung disease, from cancer to bitterness, from anger to addictions, from infections to broken bones, from mental illness to hurt feelings, we all, in some way or another, need to be healed.

But are we ready to be healed?

In my personal search for healing—and I've learned in the later years of my life that I need it in many more ways than one—I've been intrigued by what Scripture tells us about healing. We are all frequently assured that God heals, and this is true. But we seldom discuss or acknowledge what is required from us to be healed. No, it is not sinlessness, or piety, or constant striving for a perfect character. It is not a specific diet plan or a particular exercise regimen.

It is acceptance. Acceptance that God's will for us may not be our will for ourselves. Acceptance that what healing looks like to us may not be what it looks like to God—or anyone else, for that matter. Acceptance that we are in God's hands and that we belong exactly there. Acceptance that peace or forgiveness may be the healing that results from physical illness, even if that illness itself remains. Acceptance that "feeling better" may simply mean feeling closer to God and others in our lives. Acceptance that being "made whole" may have nothing to do with our bodies.

What I've also learned from Scripture and biblical healings is that we must be willing to turn to God and acknowledge our need to be healed. We must be willing to seek—and accept—God's healing, his will, for us. We must feel ourselves to be essentially valuable to God, and able to open ourselves to him, no matter how broken or ill we may be.

It is difficult to find a healing in the Bible where something is not required of the one who needs to be healed. It may be action as complicated as the friends of the paralytic in the gospel who literally took the roof off a house to lower the man in his stretcher before Jesus. It may be as simple as putting ourselves before Jesus, like the leper, and acknowledging that we know he can heal us.

In other words, healing calls for faith.

In the pages that follow, I offer the Bible passages with prayers that have helped me and others in our ongoing healing journeys. For each of the fifty-two weeks of the year, you will find a Scripture passage, a meditation and lesson, and then, a short prayer or action you can make or take for every day of every week in the year. I pray that God will bless us both with the healing we want and need on this path that ultimately can lead only to him.

HEALING DAY BY DAY

IS ANYTHING TOO WONDERFUL FOR THE LORD?

Then one said (to Abraham), "I will surely return to you in due season, and your wife Sarah shall have a son." Sarah laughed to herself. The LORD said, "Why did Sarah laugh and say to herself, 'Shall I bear a son now that I am old?' Is anything too wonderful for the LORD?" **GENESIS 18:10, 12–14**

By the time the angels of the Lord, disguised as human travelers, walked into Abraham's camp, Sarah was an old woman who thought she knew it all. She'd traveled much of the known world with Abraham, who had used her beauty when she was young to assure success and safe passage for himself. She'd left family, country, and religion to marry a man who was following the one God. She'd sacrificed everything, and though Abraham had won material success from God, Sarah had not been given what she most wanted: a son.

Sarah probably felt bitter and a little cynical when three strangers strolled into town and assured Abraham that she would bear a son. She was too old. So was he. It was ridiculous, and her laughter probably held less amusement than irony. But she was caught in her cynicism, called out by God, and—to her joy—proved wrong. She did bear a son. God healed her barrenness—the worst malady a woman of that world could face.

Do we ignore God calling us out? Do we grow so comfortable in cynicism and bitterness about our suffering that we fail to remember God's power? Have we become so accustomed to misery that it becomes habit? Are we so entrenched in complacency with our unhealed selves that we fail to properly answer the question: is anything too wonderful for the Lord? Or even to ask it?

Are we prepared to be healed?

SUNDAY ▨ *Pray:* God of all wonderful things, let me turn to you with a face shining in faith and hope rather than contorted in resentment and cynicism.

MONDAY ▨ *Act:* Today, refuse to live cynically. Think about how you regularly "act out" an attitude of surrendering hope for healing. Identify those habits that demonstrate complacency or bitterness about your situation, and banish them for twenty-four hours. Remember: nothing is impossible with God.

TUESDAY ▨ *Pray:* Lord, as you forgave Sarah for her doubtful laughter, forgive me when I refuse to acknowledge your presence and your promise.

WEDNESDAY ▨ *Act:* Throw yourself into one act of hope today. Eat healthy foods. Read an inspiring story about someone who has overcome illness or suffering. Tell someone that you believe God is healing you. Trust God!

THURSDAY ▨ *Pray:* Father, when I am afraid to hope, lest I be crushed with disappointment, remind me that one deep breath of faith in you outweighs a dozen shallow gasps of fear.

FRIDAY ▨ *Act:* Reach out to someone who is suffering and offer a reminder of God's powerful presence. Share an inspirational card, book, verse, or Scripture; or visit and simply talk about how to look for God's tree of life through a forest of worldly weeds.

SATURDAY ▨ *Pray:* Lord, remind me always about the wonderful things you have in store for me!

TOMORROW IS ANOTHER DAY

Jesus said to them, "Very truly I tell you, you will weep and mourn, but the world will rejoice; you will have pain but your pain will turn into joy." JOHN 16:19–20

When we are sick, downhearted, frightened, and in need of healing, nothing is more depressing than seeing others healthy and happy, having a great time. It's hard not to believe that they are deliberately showing off their joy and heartiness while knowing that we weep and mourn. It can feel like the world is rubbing salt in our wounds.

Jesus warned his disciples about this just before he was crucified: not only were they about to be devastated, filled with doubt and grief; they would also be forced to witness others rejoice in his death.

In times like these there is one thing we can do: remember that tomorrow is another day, and another day—or in the case of the disciples, the third day—will bring something so amazing, joyous, and unexpected that our current suffering will be removed even from memory. Indeed, Jesus goes on to assure the disciples that it will be like a woman who, once rejoicing in the birth of her child, forgets the pain of that childbirth.

My guess is that over the agonizing days after Jesus promised this joy, the disciples completely forgot his words. They were likely in shock from witnessing the swift, brutally violent end of Jesus' mission. After seeing him betrayed, denied, beaten, humiliated, condemned, crucified, and buried in a grave not his own, could they even conceive of feeling joy again?

But the day after tomorrow, they did. And so can we.

SUNDAY ▦ *Pray:* Risen Jesus, teach me to live in hope, not just for my own healing but for the joy that comes in knowing that you conquered sin, pain, and death, once and for all.

MONDAY ▦ *Act:* Think about the last time you felt joy. Consider the feeling and the reason for it. Now think back again. Was there a time before that joyful period that you felt pain? Of course there was. Remember that if your pain turned to joy in the past, it will do so again.

TUESDAY ▦ *Pray:* Jesus, when I weep let my tears wash away the pain and grief so that I may raise my dim eyes to the east in hope.

WEDNESDAY ▦ *Act:* Make a list of ways in which the pain you now feel might be turned to joy. Lift this list to God in openhearted, trusting prayer.

THURSDAY ▦ *Pray:* Enduring Jesus, help me wait patiently and faithfully until you turn my tears of pain into rejoicing.

FRIDAY ▦ *Act:* Spend time—in person, over the phone, by e-mail, or through a letter or card—with someone experiencing pain or grief. Without belittling their suffering, gently let them know that "this, too, will pass."

SATURDAY ▦ *Pray:* Lord, thank you for every new dawn with its promise of relief, healing, and rejoicing.

SEEK HELP WITH A RIGHT HEART

Esau said to Jacob, "Let me eat some of that, for I am famished!"
Jacob said, "First sell me your birthright." Esau said, "I am about
to die; of what use is a birthright to me?" So he swore to him and
sold his birthright to Jacob. **GENESIS 25:30–33**

E sau is a perfect example of what not to do when illness and discomfort overwhelm us. Weak and sick with hunger, he grasps at the first thing that comes his way that appears to offer relief. He is so desperate that he doesn't stop to think of the cost of this "remedy." He doesn't consider whether he is seeking God's help or settling for a worldly "cure" that requires him to turn away from God. By rejecting God's gift to him—being the firstborn—Esau chooses a "quick fix" over gratitude and trust in God.

It is easy to react to suffering the way Esau reacts. We just want the torment to stop; we just want to feel better. And we want it now. We want relief in our time, on our terms, regardless of what God wants or might be trying to teach us through our pain.

Was it wrong for Esau to want food to relieve and sustain him? No. But when Jacob told Esau that he could only have the food if he turned away from God and God's gift, Esau should have chosen to endure until he could get food for which he could thank God and consume with a righteous heart.

So, are we to reject anything that might help us? Again, no. But before seeking remedies, we should remember that all means to health come from God and thank him for providing the benefits of medicine, food, exercise, technology. All true healing flows from God, and without God, nothing we consume will help.

SUNDAY ■ *Pray:* God of all cures, when I desperately want relief from my pain, remind me to first turn to you, not only for physical healing but for peace and comfort.

MONDAY ■ *Act:* Whatever you plan to consume today to give you relief—an aspirin, an antidepressant, chemo, a nutritional supplement, any medicine or food—take time first to thank God for the gift of this substance. Ask God to bless this medicine.

TUESDAY ■ *Pray:* Lord, give me the discernment to know what is good for me—that is, what is from you.

WEDNESDAY ■ *Act:* If you have been suffering for any length of time, it is likely that others have given you advice. Before taking any advice, run it by God. Bring the suggestions of others to God in prayer, remembering that while others may have good intentions, their intentions are human. God's are divine.

THURSDAY ■ *Pray:* O Great Physician, please bless my efforts to help myself, reminding me that I can do nothing without you

FRIDAY ■ *Act:* Examine your motives before advising someone in need of healing. Are you suggesting a particular course of action because it is one you've chosen and you want the affirmation of knowing that others support your decision?

SATURDAY ■ *Pray:* Lord, remind me that, before I advise others, I would do well to first seek your counsel.

RECOGNIZE YOUR HEALER

Just then there was in their synagogue a man with an unclean spirit, and he cried out, "What have you to do with us, Jesus of Nazareth? I know who you are, the Holy One of God." But Jesus rebuked him, saying, "Be silent, and come out of him!" **MARK 1:23–25**

C ould it be that even the sickness that seems to have a grip on us is longing to be healed? Do the things that need healing in us recognize that Jesus is the ultimate healer even before we manage to understand this?

In this and other Scripture passages, the dis-eases that possess various people recognize Jesus, and not only do these illnesses recognize Jesus, they seek attention from him. They identify him for all to hear, thus drawing all attention to themselves. Knowing full well that Jesus has the power to banish them, these illnesses call out to him, almost daring him to do so! In this gospel, the man who is ill doesn't even seem to know that Jesus is there, or understand who Jesus is. There is no indication that he, himself, has come to Jesus to be healed. But the sickness within him knows that Jesus has the power to heal, has power over all dis-ease. Thus, the people witnessing this particular healing murmur, "He commands even the unclean spirits, and they obey him" (Mark 1:27).

The power of God to heal is so profound that we may instinctually know it deep within ourselves, even deep within our woundedness—or perhaps most strongly within our woundedness—before we can fully comprehend it in a rational, conscious way. The illness within us can't help itself: it calls out to the healer.

We must, consciously and deliberately, do the same.

SUNDAY ▦ *Pray:* Lord, even as every cell in my body and every part of my spirit instinctively cry out to you for healing, let my ears and brain and mouth hear and comprehend and pray.

MONDAY ▦ *Act:* Consciously recognize Jesus in your health practices. Before you do your exercises, think about all the walking Jesus did throughout Palestine as he healed in every town and city. Before you take your medicine or vitamins or health supplements, remember how Jesus ate and drank with those he'd healed.

TUESDAY ▦ *Pray:* Jesus, forgive me for all the times my mind and eyes are closed to your healing presence in my life, even in the midst of my sickness.

WEDNESDAY ▦ *Act:* Before you read an article on illness or the instructions accompanying a medicine or prescription, or before you go online to research a health issue, go first to your Bible and read a gospel account of Jesus' healing power.

THURSDAY ▦ *Pray:* Lord, help me to identify the parts of me that need to be healed and to turn them over to you.

FRIDAY ▦ *Act:* Make a different kind of health care appointment: find out when there is a healing service in your parish or at another area congregation; make a commitment to attend.

SATURDAY ▦ *Pray:* Powerful Lord, cast out from me any spirit of blindness or obstinance so that I may perceive and feel your power at work in me always.

PHYSICAL REMINDERS OF HEALING

He struck him on the hip socket; and Jacob's hip was put out of joint as he wrestled with him. The sun rose upon (Jacob) as he passed Penuel, limping because of his hip. GENESIS 32:25, 31

We are conditioned to think of scars or other visible remnants of past illness as negative or unattractive. We don't want to see these signs of sickness. They remind us of the pain, uncertainty, and weakness we felt at that time. And they are a constant and noticeable intimation that we are still vulnerable, that we could become sick again.

But Jacob has earned his limp, and he does not despise it. He has spent an entire night wrestling with a mysterious man, perhaps an angel who represents God, and Jacob does not give up until his adversary strikes him on the hip, thus leaving him with a visible and painful reminder of the encounter. The limp is also a reminder that Jacob refused to surrender until he received a blessing from the man of God. We can almost see Jacob limping, a little proudly, toward the dawn of the new day and a new life, blessed by God. He was sick with worry and fear about his future, and the encounter freed him from that anxiety, leaving him with a physical manifestation of that healing.

Jacob will go on to live a long, fruitful life, which will also be fraught with danger and fear. It's easy to imagine him as he ages and faces many challenges as the patriarch of a new nation blessed by God. Occasionally he will feel a twinge of pain from that wrestling match. When the weather changes, he'll limp a little. And probably when he does, he'll smile a little too.

SUNDAY ▪ *Pray:* God of Israel, help me to bear confidently the scars and manifestations of past illnesses, knowing that you marked me with your blessing.

MONDAY ▪ *Act:* Study yourself in a mirror. Do you have visible signs of a past illness or disability? Can you see indications of aging or the worries you've faced? Try to see these scars or wrinkles or glasses not as ugly or anxiety-making but as manifestations of how God has healed you and is healing you.

TUESDAY ▪ *Pray:* Father, teach me to see myself with a fraction of the compassion and love that you see me with.

WEDNESDAY ▪ *Act:* Do you occasionally—perhaps more often than you'd like—feel an ache or pain that is "left over" from an earlier illness or injury? Promise yourself today that the next time you feel this pain, you will perceive it not as a sign of your weakness but of God's strength.

THURSDAY ▪ *Pray:* Almighty God, show me how to accept my old "war wounds" as a reminder of how you fight—and win—for me.

FRIDAY ▪ *Act:* Do you know someone who is visibly scarred? Have you ever turned away from that person or privately thought him or her unattractive? Ask God to forgive your miscomprehension. When you next see that person, be ready with a sincere, heartfelt greeting.

SATURDAY ▪ *Pray:* Father, forgive me when I fail to see your perfection in my imperfections.

HEALING THE SICKNESS OF ANGER

"So when you are offering your gift at the altar, if you remember that your brother or sister has something against you...first be reconciled to your brother or sister, and then come and offer your gift." MATTHEW 5:23–24

J esus is telling us that we can't be "right" or healthy before God until and unless we are healed in our relationships. Modern medical science and psychology tell us many things—often conflicting—about anger. Some say it is healthy and must be expressed. Some say it is damaging and must be controlled. But either way, Jesus, as always, has the last and correct word: unaddressed anger is a canker sore on our relationships with each other, and on our bond with God, who asks us to love and care for one another.

Jesus points out that we can't "heal" the damage done by anger by donating to the church, giving to others, and leading a "good" life by outward appearances. All of these are false if we do them just "for show" while we secretly seethe or cause others to be enraged with us. We ignore the sickness of anger at our own peril, not to mention the peril of those involved in our anger or those who are angry at us.

We cannot be "right" with God if we are deliberately and knowingly "wrong" with another. Jesus summarized his entire body of teachings by telling us to love God and love one another. He was born to show that it was no longer enough to do the first without at least trying to do the second.

Yet it can be difficult to "be reconciled" as Jesus instructs, particularly if the conflict is long-standing or deeply personal. We need to first ask the Lord for help. We must ask for the grace to do what we can't do without grace: forgive, and ask for forgiveness.

SUNDAY *Pray:* Jesus, you were born and died for forgiveness. Give me strength to seek it from you and from others, and to give it whenever I can.

MONDAY *Act:* Forgive a stranger—perhaps the guy who cut you off in traffic, the woman at the grocery store who loudly commented on your Ben & Jerry's addiction, the trash collector who left your bin in the street. These are all your brothers and sisters.

TUESDAY *Pray:* Lord, help me to remember that with you, I can't pretend everything is all right. I cannot hide my anger from you.

WEDNESDAY *Act:* Forgive a colleague—maybe the committee chair who dismissed your suggestion, the supervisor who gave you a lukewarm review, the coach who yelled at your child during practice. Forgiving does not mean you agree with hurtful actions but that you won't be hurtful in return.

THURSDAY *Pray:* Jesus, teach me to truly repent of the wrongs I have done to others, in preparation for "doing right" by them.

FRIDAY *Act:* Forgive a loved one. Whether your spouse forgot an important occasion, your child said something hurtful, or your best friend criticized you, seek true reconciliation. Have an honest but loving encounter, and no matter how your loved one reacts, release yourself from the sickness of anger.

SATURDAY *Pray:* Lord, you forgave your tormentors and murderers from the cross; let me lay down my cross of anger so as to better help carry yours.

SEEKING GOD'S HELP

When the cloud went away from over the tent, Miriam had become leprous, as white as snow. And Moses cried out to the LORD, "O God, please heal her." NUMBERS 12:10, 13

It seems like common sense that we should automatically turn to God for healing. After all, we know that in God resides the ultimate power to heal, to give life, to raise from the dead. So why do we hesitate sometimes? Why are our prayers halfhearted or uncertain? Could it be that we are not sure we deserve God's healing help?

In this Scripture, it is interesting to note that Miriam herself does not ask for God's help. Nor does her devastated brother, Aaron. They turn to Moses and ask him to call upon the Lord for healing. Miriam and Aaron know they have sinned against God by envying Moses and trying to possess some of the power God gave him. It seems, therefore, that they don't dare to directly approach God for healing.

We can sometimes feel the same way, not daring to ask for God's healing, to "bother" God, especially when we know how we have failed him and continue to fail him through sin and our human nature. We fear, sometimes even subconsciously, that we are not worthy to ask God for help.

Here's the (sort of) good news: no one is worthy of God. It is impossible for a human being to be worthy of God, or to "earn" God's love or intercession or healing. Miriam had Moses, but we have an even greater intercessor: Jesus, who, through grace that he makes accessible to all who believe in him, can and does approach God for us and with us. Jesus knows how much the Father loves us, even when we don't.

SUNDAY ▓ *Pray:* Gracious God, healer of Miriam even after she transgressed against you and Moses, help me to put aside my fear and shame and to approach you with heart and body ready to seek and receive your healing.

MONDAY ▓ *Act:* Focus on a saint who had the courage to seek God even after sinning. There are many! Augustine, David, Dorothy Day, Paul, etc. Consider how this holy person has acknowledged sinning against God. Understand that you have done nothing worse than these, and yet these became God's own messengers. You can do the same.

TUESDAY ▓ *Pray:* Jesus, give me the courage to rely on your grace as I come before you in prayer for healing.

WEDNESDAY ▓ *Act:* Do something today to show repentance for the sin or sins that hold you back from seeking God's grace and healing.

THURSDAY ▓ *Pray:* Lord, take away any fears or feelings of shame that keep me from turning to you for help.

FRIDAY ▓ *Act:* Offer to pray with someone who needs healing. If that person is fearful of God, and thus hampered in prayer, take the lead as Moses did for Miriam and help her or him find their way back to God.

SATURDAY ▓ *Pray:* Merciful Father, I trust in your power to heal and love me, even when I don't trust in my own ability to fully open myself to your grace.

Week Eight

COMING TO HIM

---

*So his fame spread throughout all Syria, and they brought to him
all the sick, those who were afflicted with various diseases and
pains...and he cured them.* MATTHEW 4:24

When we are ill, we go the Internet, we go to medical books, we go to the doctor, the physical therapist, the pharmacist, the psychologist, the surgeon. But do we go to God? And if we go to God, when do we go to God?

Is our first thought to turn to God? Is our first action to ask God for help? Or do we wait until after we've made the doctor's appointment, filled the prescription, and checked a few websites? Worse, do we wait until nothing else has worked to make us better...and only then remember God?

Jesus' reputation as a healer grew rapidly in the Middle East of those times, but one of the most notable things about the vast majority of his healings is that the sick either came to him, or others brought them to him—as is the case in the gospel passage above—or they begged him to come to them. We seldom see Jesus, out of the blue, deciding to heal someone who hasn't asked for healing.

Does this means that Jesus didn't enjoy healing or lacked the compassion to heal without being asked? Of course not! It may mean that Jesus, who was with God as co-creator, knew his creatures even while living among and as one of them. He knew that for healing to be complete, we must at the very least acknowledge that we need him to heal us. He doesn't need to come to us, because he is always with us. But we do need to come to him if for no other reason than to recognize his healing presence.

SUNDAY   *Pray:* Lord, whether I am "brought" to you by others or whether I bring myself, help me to willingly come to you for healing.

MONDAY   *Act:* "Bring" yourself to God today for healing. Whether to a church, other sacred place, or even the quiet of your room where you have experienced God in the past, actually go to that place and quietly present yourself to God in your brokenness and need.

TUESDAY   *Pray:* Jesus, as I do all the practical, worldly things that I believe are necessary to get better, let me keep your name and power first and foremost in my mind and on my lips.

WEDNESDAY   *Act:* Research people who take pilgrimages to bring themselves before God for healing. People make great sacrifices, financial and otherwise, to make these journeys to Lourdes and other renowned healing places. Make your own personal, private sacrifice today as you come to the Lord for healing.

THURSDAY   *Pray:* Compassionate Jesus, remind me to come to you when I need spiritual and emotional healing as well as physical healing.

FRIDAY   *Act:* Matthew describes how others "brought" the sick to Jesus. Offer to bring someone to a medical appointment and use the traveling time to pray with that person, thus bringing him or her first to the Lord.

SATURDAY   *Pray:* Lord, once I have come to you, give me the patience to wait for your healing.

Week Nine

ASK RIGHTLY

---

*The elders of Israel...said to Samuel, "Appoint for us a king
to govern us, like other nations." The LORD said to Samuel,
"You shall solemnly warn them and show them the ways of
the king who shall reign over them." But the people refused to
listen; they said, "No! but we are determined to have a king."*
1 SAMUEL 8:5, 7, 9, 19

The Israelites come to Samuel demanding a king because they want to be like other nations; they want to "heal" their differentness instead of celebrating the fact that they are different because God—and no mere man—is their king. God, seemingly perceiving this demand as a rejection, instructs Samuel to warn them about human kings.

As the First Book of Samuel continues, God gives the Israelites exactly what they ask for, thus beginning the long decline, dissolution, and eventual division of the country and the people. With the exception of David and, occasionally, Solomon, the kings of Israel—and later of Israel and Judah, once they divide—are mostly petty, greedy, venal, and not in good standing with God.

The people ask for the wrong kind of healing, a healing that flies in the face of God and expresses ingratitude and callousness toward the Lord. And when they get it, they find themselves more sick than they could have ever imagined. Indeed, they find themselves eventually destroyed as a coherent nation.

How often do we ask God for a "healing"—a solution to dis-ease—that we are absolutely convinced will do the trick in our lives, fixing every problem, making us feel instantly better about ourselves and the world? How often do we ignore God's warnings about this thing we ask for? How often do we blame God if he doesn't give it to us, rather than thanking him for saving us from ourselves?

SUNDAY *Pray:* Lord, teach me to ask only for what is good for me in your eyes.

MONDAY *Act:* Make two columns. On one side, list past wishes that you thought you absolutely had to have, listing only fulfilled wishes. On the other side, note the results (or consequences) of receiving those desires. Did any of those wishes end up not being as wonderful for you as you'd thought?

TUESDAY *Pray:* Father, when I cannot discern the kind of healing I really need, help me to rely on your mercy to make me whole in the ways that you choose.

WEDNESDAY *Act:* List all the ways in which you want God to "heal" you today. Carefully examine those things that you would ask God for. Are there ways in which some of them might not work toward healing and wholeness?

THURSDAY *Pray:* Loving God, when, in my ignorance, I pray for that which will not heal or help me, mercifully deny my prayer.

FRIDAY *Act:* Is someone you know praying for something that may not help them? If you have a strong relationship, compassionately suggest that this specific wish may not bring true healing. If you don't have that kind of relationship, pray that God will gently enlighten him or her.

SATURDAY *Pray:* Lord, lead me to trust always that you—and you alone—know what I need and will grant it to me in your own time.

Week Ten

WORRYING DOESN'T HELP...OR HEAL

"And can any of you by worrying add a single hour to your span of life? So do not worry about tomorrow, for tomorrow will bring worries of its own. Today's trouble is enough for today."
MATTHEW 6:27, 34

I am an inveterate worrier, but as I get older, what I've started to worry about most is how my worrying not only makes things worse but also temporarily blinds me to God's grace and presence in my life. This passage from Matthew is only one of several instances where Jesus warns us against worry. Note that he doesn't say we have nothing to worry about. As both God and man, Jesus knows full well that we have plenty to worry about in our sad and often hurt world. So he doesn't hum a little tune and tell us that everything's just hunky-dory.

Instead, Jesus points out, in a way that is more practical than obviously spiritual, that worrying accomplishes nothing. It doesn't even take away the worry that tomorrow will bring more worries! It only adds to that burdensome reality.

In my experience, worrying can make illness or dis-ease even worse. Studies show this to be true: stress and worry weaken the immune system and make it more difficult to get well and stay well.

The context of this quote by Jesus is a longer talk in which he encourages the disciples and listeners not to despair because worry begets worry, but to understand that God is in charge; the Father will take care of us, heal us, in his own time and place. Worrying, especially absent positive action, will not hasten healing. And in my own life, I have come to wonder if worrying in the face of God isn't a small disappointment to him.

SUNDAY ▨ *Pray:* Wise Jesus, remind me that it was in the midst of your own difficult life as a human that you were still able to encourage us not to worry.

MONDAY ▨ *Act:* What are you most worried about today? List any practical, positive actions you can take, with prayer and God's help, to address this issue. Begin to take these actions, understanding that worrying is not one of them.

TUESDAY ▨ *Pray:* Lord, when I feel overwhelmed by anxiety, help me to remember that you suffered and died to show me how much you and the Father love me.

WEDNESDAY ▨ *Act:* Take a walk! Walking, or any moderate exercise, releases endorphins into your system that can help lift your spirit toward God and away from worry. If you cannot exercise at all, try reading a good book, doing a crossword or other puzzle, or playing a word or board game that requires concentration…and that might just be fun!

THURSDAY ▨ *Pray:* Father, let me release my worries into your kind care, knowing that only in you will I find true peace.

FRIDAY ▨ *Act:* Reach out to someone who is worried. Share with them the good news of this gospel, pray with them for a release from worry and the condition that is causing it, and do something fun or interesting to distract them.

SATURDAY ▨ *Pray:* Merciful Lord, forgive me for the times that worry has blinded me to your great love and powerful presence.

IT WILL BE ALL RIGHT

She called to her husband, and said, "Send me one of the servants and one of the donkeys, so that I may go quickly to the man of God." He said, "Why go today?" She said, "It will be all right."
2 KINGS 4:22–23

I nstead of telling her husband the truth—that their young son has died in her arms and that she is going to find Elisha, the man of God, for that reason—the Shunammitess of the Bible tells her elderly husband, with whom she has only this one son: "It will be all right."

Is she deliberately lying to him?

Later, when Elisha's servant, Gehazi, comes to meet her and asks if she and her husband and her son are all right, she responds, "It is all right."

Is she deliberately lying to him?

It is only when she comes to Elisha, through whom God has given her this cherished, late-in-life son, that she explains what has happened and expresses her utter determination that Elisha should come and heal her child. Which he does.

Does the Shunammitess believe herself when she tells her husband and Gehazi that everything is all right? Does she expect a miracle? Or is she delusional, trying to comfort herself or even deny the reality of her child's death? Or does she realize that God, through Elisha, has given her this child; and so God, through Elisha, can give him back to her alive and well?

Is she, then, an Old Testament embodiment of Jesus' assurance that when we ask for something with complete confidence and faith in God, we will receive what we need? Does she have that kind of faith?

Do we?

SUNDAY ▓ *Pray:* Lord, strengthen my faith! Even when I doubt myself and others, let me never doubt the magnitude of your power.

MONDAY ▓ *Act:* After making a request to God in prayer, act as if your prayer has been answered. Live your answered prayer as fully as you physically, emotionally, and spiritually can. Now live it more fully, exceeding your own ability by relying on God's grace. Reject any possibility other than answered prayer.

TUESDAY ▓ *Pray:* Father, confident in my faith, I thank you in advance for answering my prayer.

WEDNESDAY ▓ *Act:* Encourage yourself by reading accounts of saints and martyrs who have asked God for the seemingly impossible and, believing, received what they requested. Start with Jesus, who, while asking God to forgive those who were torturing and murdering him, obtained God's forgiveness for the whole world!

THURSDAY ▓ *Pray:* God, grant me the faith to pray faithfully, and the confidence in you to pray confidently.

FRIDAY ▓ *Act:* Just as Elisha was God's agent, look for ways that God can work through you to answer another's prayer. Is someone praying for an end to loneliness? A respite from caring for a loved one? A little extra money for pressing bills? Someone to run an errand? Be God's answer.

SATURDAY ▓ *Pray:* Lord, when I am questioned about myself, let me answer: "It is all right," or, "It will be all right." And let me believe it.

Week Twelve

I DO CHOOSE

And there was a leper who came to him and knelt before him, saying, "Lord, if you choose, you can make me clean." He stretched out his hand and touched him, saying, "I do choose. Be made clean!" MATTHEW 8:2–3

These few lines in Matthew contain enough insight and truth about God's healing power to fill volumes! This leper, rejected by society, forced to live on the margins, unwelcome in any home or place of worship, surviving off the scraps of the community, understands in an instant what most of us spend our entire lives trying to grasp. Jesus has the power to do anything he chooses to do, including, and especially, healing.

The leper doesn't even ask Jesus to heal him. He simply observes the majesty and extent of Jesus' power: "If you choose, you can make me clean." The leper knows he doesn't need to get to what we call "the asking." His faith is astonishing. And it affects Jesus deeply; this is one of the few gospel passages where Jesus responds to a request with an exclamation: I do choose. Be made clean! Jesus responds in language almost exactly like the leper's. The Lord recognizes that this wretched man gets it, gets him, and he responds accordingly.

How I wish I had the leper's faith! How I wish I had the faith to say, in effect, Lord, I know you can heal me. Period. Instead, I'm more likely to reel off my laundry list for the day and then beg and plead, in great detail with many specifics, about just what I want healed of and how. And, of course, always now!

Two thousand years later, many of us are still working on what that leper, in his misery and isolation, had already achieved.

SUNDAY ▧ *Pray:* Lord, if you choose, you can make me more faithful.

MONDAY ▧ *Act:* Deliberately keep God's healing power in mind today. Consider its magnificence and magnitude. Understand that you really can't completely comprehend it. Accept that it is beyond imagining but always accessible. Every time you start to ask God for something, stop and, instead, make a reverent acknowledgment of God's power to do anything…and more.

TUESDAY ▧ *Pray:* Lord, if you choose, you can heal all of my ills and dis-eases.

WEDNESDAY ▧ *Act:* Be conscious of the many specific ways that God's healing power works in your life. Every step you take is because God has made your body a mobile miracle. Every pill, vitamin, or supplement you swallow was created from substances God put in the world and through the intelligence God gave researchers. Every organ that works properly was fashioned to work that way by God. Be aware that God's power is everywhere, in everything, in you.

THURSDAY ▧ *Pray:* Lord, if you choose, you can free me from my fears.

FRIDAY ▧ *Act:* Reflect the leper's faith back to others today. Look for opportunities to remark on God's power. "May God keep you in good health!" "God has you looking well today." "Thank God you can see so well with your new glasses!" "God blessed us with a beautiful day for a walk."

SATURDAY ▧ *Pray:* Lord, if you choose, you can remove any obstacles I've foolishly placed in the path to you.

ACKNOWLEDGING OUR ROLE
IN SICKNESS AND HEALTH

The people came to Moses and said, "We have sinned by speaking against the LORD and against you; pray to the LORD to take away the serpents from us." So Moses prayed. And the LORD said to Moses, "Make a serpent and set it on a pole; and everyone who is bitten shall look at it and live." NUMBERS 21:7–8

I t's hard to admit, or sometimes even to recognize, but there are times when we are complicit in our own sickness. We put ourselves in situations where we are likely to become sick, dis-eased, or troubled. We allow ourselves to be tempted to do things that are not healthy for us, physically, emotionally, or spiritually. We make choices that invite or prolong illness.

In this Scripture, the Israelites have again offended God, and God has responded by sending serpents to plague and kill them. Again they ask Moses to pray for them. Again Moses appeals to God. Again God forgives and heals them. Yet in healing them, God reminds them of their complicity in this plague of death and illness. In being healed, they are not allowed to forget how they brought this upon themselves, because to be healed, they must look upon the very symbol of their punishment. They are being attacked by serpents, and so God decrees that they must look upon a serpent, thus confronting their own role in this sickness.

No one can probe the thoughts of God, but there may be a component of compassion in this punishment. Perhaps if the Israelites are forced to confront their own reckless rejection of God—the cure being a symbol of the punishment—they will be less likely to repeat this foolish act.

Are we aware of the ways in which we reject God's gift of health? Or do we just want him to heal us without helping us?

SUNDAY ■ *Pray:* Lord, when I seek your healing, let me prepare by addressing whether I have exacerbated my own unhealthiness.

MONDAY ■ *Act:* Consider your most troubling dis-ease. Are there choices or habits through which you are complicit in this problem? Do you do anything to worsen or prolong it? Do you avoid choices that you know will support good health? Make a list of these, and read it daily to increase your awareness.

TUESDAY ■ *Pray:* Compassionate Father, give me courage to confront my illness and avail myself of the resources you provide.

WEDNESDAY ■ *Act:* Select one behavior from Monday's list and address it. If you've avoided a medical appointment, make (and keep!) it. If you drink too much, cut down and get help. If you need exercise, get moving!

THURSDAY ■ *Pray:* Great God, help me to recognize and stop behaviors that disrespect your gifts of my body and mind.

FRIDAY ■ *Act:* Try to help someone who is complicit in his or her unhealthiness. Instead of bringing an overweight family member candy or food, bring flowers or a book. If your child has an attention disorder, turn off all televisions and electronics for an hour each evening to help him or her concentrate on homework. Meet your diabetic friend for a light lunch instead of coffee and dessert.

SATURDAY ■ *Pray:* Lord, open my eyes to the ways in which you teach me healthy behaviors.

HUMILITY IN SEEKING TO BE HEALED

A centurion came to him...saying, "Lord, my servant is lying at home paralyzed, in terrible distress." And Jesus said, "I will come and cure him." The centurion answered, "Lord, I am not worthy to have you come under my roof; but only speak the word, and my servant will be healed." **MATTHEW 8:5–8**

Many of those who show the strongest faith in Jesus' healing powers are outsiders: lepers, tax collectors, prostitutes, Canaanites, Samaritans, and now this centurion, a highly placed soldier from the despised Roman oppressors.

Yet, these most despised and rejected come to Jesus with heart-wrenching humility, desperate for the smallest bit of his time and power, unwaveringly certain of his miracle-working capabilities. The centurion believes that just by saying a word—one word!—and that word from a long distance, Jesus will heal a beloved servant.

So it is today. From the very poor, the addicted, the seriously ill, people with AIDS, the homeless—those rejected and abandoned by "normal," "healthy" society—I am often humbled to hear words of faith and confidence in God so heartfelt that they sometimes put me to shame. I have a friend who has struggled all his life with financial, health, and addiction issues whose son is now lying in a state-run facility dying of congenital heart disease. "The Lord will take care of us," he assures me. "I trust him."

Matthew tells us that after hearing the words of the centurion, Jesus is amazed and exclaims, "In no one in Israel have I found such faith" (Matthew 8:10).

Wouldn't it be wonderful to amaze the Lord with our faith?

SUNDAY   *Pray:* Amazing Jesus, help me to believe and know in my very bones that you need only say the word, and I will be healed.

MONDAY   *Act:* Approach the Lord for healing as the centurion does. Lead with humility and faith. Write your request in just a few words and leave the page by a cross or in your Bible on the page of Matthew, Chapter 8. Present this simple prayer to God.

TUESDAY   *Pray:* Lord, let me approach you without ego, pride, or sense of achievement. I humble myself before you in supplication.

WEDNESDAY   *Act:* Imagine that you have no formal standing before God. You don't belong to or attend a church, and no one knows you as a Christian. Imagine that you are poor, disabled, unemployed, a member of a mistrusted minority. Imagine that you are homeless, hungry, cold, confused, angry. Imagine that, despite all this, you have come to believe that God, and God alone, can heal. Now, bring your request to him.

THURSDAY   *Pray:* Gracious Father, teach me that no matter how high I rise in the estimation of others, I can only honestly approach you on my knees.

FRIDAY   *Act:* Donate clean blankets, towels, clothes, toiletries, and healthy food to your church's pantry for the poor or to a local homeless shelter or soup kitchen.

SATURDAY   *Pray:* Lord, let me prepare myself for your healing by understanding that I cannot earn it; I can only have faith in it.

GOD NEEDS NO DRAMA

―――――――――

Elisha sent a message..."Go, wash in the Jordan seven times, and your flesh shall be restored and you shall be clean." But Naaman became angry...saying, "I thought that for me surely he would come out, and stand and call on the name of the LORD his God, and would wave his hand over the spot and cure the leprosy!" 2 KINGS 5:10–11

When we are ill, it is often all we can think about. Every aspect, symptom, twinge, and pain registers in our consciousness, increasing the burden and depth of our distress. Our anxiety grows, and with it every symptom becomes literally and figuratively more intense and noticeable. It is the proverbial vicious cycle.

Illness is our own personal drama.

And we want a big, dramatic cure. We want God to change everything overnight; never mind overnight, in an instant would be even better. We want the pain, the symptoms, the illness to be gone, and not only those, but the memory of them and the vulnerability that came with them.

After all, aren't we worthy? Aren't we special? Don't we obey the rules, say our prayers, do what we're supposed to do? Aren't we important enough? Naaman surely thought he was.

I think it unlikely that God smiles upon the webs of drama and self-importance we weave around ourselves. I think a little humility and patience and retrospection may be more in line with his hopes for us. It is interesting that it was Naaman's servants—those accustomed to humility, patience, silence—who talked him into following Elisha's advice. When Naaman did put aside his own drama and follow their advice to humbly wash in the Jordan, God healed him.

SUNDAY ▦ *Pray:* Lord, lift me out of the dreadful drama of illness and calm my heart to await your healing power.

MONDAY ▦ *Act:* Naaman initially ignored the advice of Elisha, God's prophet. Are there "prophets" and messengers in your life whom you ignore? Think about someone who has given you simple, spiritual, godly advice in the past that you initially dismissed. Can you seek that person's advice now? If not, how do you think she or he would counsel you?

TUESDAY ▦ *Pray:* Father, give me the discernment and humility to listen to those you send, especially when they give me calming, simple, sensible advice.

WEDNESDAY ▦ *Act:* Take time off from the drama of your illness. To the extent that you are able, do any or all of the following: take slow, deep breaths, clearing your mind as best you can; practice centering prayer, yoga, gentle stretches, tai chi; watch an engrossing movie; read or listen to a good book; lose yourself in a magazine or journal article on an interesting topic.

THURSDAY ▦ *Pray:* Merciful God, teach me that in sickness and in health, I must adjust myself to your plan and schedule rather than expect you to adjust to mine.

FRIDAY ▦ *Act:* Be a calm, clear voice for someone struggling with the panic and drama of illness. Speak gently, firmly, practically, and encouragingly. Offer hope. Counsel patience. Pray.

SATURDAY ▦ *Pray:* Lord, in the midst of my sickness, open my eyes to the lessons you are offering me.

Week Sixteen

SERVE HIM

When Jesus entered Peter's house, he saw his mother-in-law lying in bed with a fever; he touched her hand, and the fever left her, and she got up and began to serve him. **MATTHEW 8:14–15**

I t is not so surprising that when Jesus sees the mother-in-law of his right-hand guy, Peter, the rock, the one he would choose to lead the church, he heals her. After all, he heals myriad strangers, why not someone "in the family"? In fact, it's easy to imagine that whenever Jesus visited the home of an apostle or disciple, those in that home were healed "automatically," in a matter of speaking, by his very presence. They probably don't need to express their faith or even ask to be healed. Right?

Or is it that their faith is so profound, so confident, so complete, that it is not so much unexpressed but inexpressible. Jesus knows it, feels it. And he heals, forgives, sanctifies simply because he is...and because he is with them in the presence of such faith.

His healing of Peter's mother-in-law stands out not because it is dramatic or because she and her family come to Jesus for healing, like many who are healed in the gospels, but because they don't. And there is something even more important about this healing. She got up and began to serve him. The matriarch of Peter's household knows instantly what to do.

All in perfect, faithful silence. The expectation of healing is present. The faith to be healed is present. The gratitude is present. The response to Jesus in the form of service is present. And no one has to say a word.

SUNDAY ▦ *Pray:* Jesus, even as I remain in need of healing, help me to give my life, broken as it may be, into your service.

MONDAY ▦ *Act:* Serve God even before you are healed. No matter how small, there is some way to serve. Offer a kind word of thanks or encouragement to your caretaker(s). Compliment the nurse at the doctor's office or hospital. Write or e-mail someone who needs to hear from you. Find a way to serve in your brokenness.

TUESDAY ▦ *Pray:* Lord, let my faith be so strong and steadfast that it may also be, occasionally, silent.

WEDNESDAY ▦ *Act:* Invite Jesus into your home. Though you are in need of healing, don't invite him so that he will heal you. Invite him because you love him and want to know him better, because you'd like to share a meal with him. Invite Jesus today and serve him as your guest.

THURSDAY ▦ *Pray:* Compassionate Jesus! Please come into the place where I dwell and, by your very presence, heal my languishing body and spirit!

FRIDAY ▦ *Act:* Bring Jesus into the home of someone who is sick. Visit with a Bible, book, or video about Jesus that you can share. Read aloud gospel passages about Jesus' healing powers. Talk about Jesus and what it means to invite him into one's life.

SATURDAY ▦ *Pray:* Lord, shower me with your grace so that I, too, may be a member of your family and serve you in my home and yours.

GOD WORKS IN MYSTERIOUS WAYS

The word of the Lord came to (Isaiah): "...say to Hezekiah, prince of my people, Thus says the LORD, the God of your ancestor, David: I have heard your prayer...indeed I will heal you." Then Isaiah said, "Bring a lump of figs...apply it to the boil, so that he may recover."
2 KINGS 20:4, 5, 7

P oor King Hezekiah must have felt stranded between the sublime and the ridiculous. Previously God told him, through Isaiah, that he was about to die. But Hezekiah implores God for healing, and God rewards his faith by not only promising to heal him but by adding fifteen years to his life and freeing him from the conquering Assyrians! Talk about sublime!

Then, when God is apparently finished speaking through Isaiah, the prophet turns to the assembled servants and physicians and orders that a bunch of figs be stuck to the king's sore "so that he may recover."

Ridiculous?

Not really.

Did God heal Hezekiah or was it the figs?

Yes.

It may be a bit of a shock to think of God offering Hezekiah magnificent healing, extended life, and astounding military victory, all to be wrapped in a poultice of boiled figs. But it shouldn't be. God made the earth and everything in it to work toward—and to be made to work toward—our well-being. The difficult part sometimes is to remember—even without a grand pronouncement—that God is behind every good thing in our lives.

Hezekiah probably wasn't surprised at all about the figs. He understood that the Lord had already done those things he'd promised; the figs were simply a God-given means to a God-given end.

SUNDAY ■ *Pray:* Gracious God, I praise and thank you for the many means to physical and spiritual healing that you provide.

MONDAY ■ *Act:* Got figs? Figs are among the many healthy things God has created. Get some figs, give thanks to God for them, and eat up.

TUESDAY ■ *Pray:* Lord, help me to recognize the humble materials you offer for my healing when I search with eyes opened by faith.

WEDNESDAY ■ *Act:* When you give thanks for your meals today, give thanks also for the many healing properties of the food God has provided. Observe that the simpler (and more humble) the food, quite often the greater its benefits. Be aware of this as you choose what to eat, and be grateful for the knowledge God provides.

THURSDAY ■ *Pray:* Lord, let me be like Hezekiah and turn to you in all humility, knowing that you are the only one able to heal me, free me, and take me in your due time, unto yourself.

FRIDAY ■ *Act:* Bring or send healthy food or food-based medicines to a homeless shelter or soup kitchen. Frequently the poorest among us are those with the least access to healthy foods, so you can be God's agent in making this gift.

SATURDAY ■ *Pray:* Father, give me the grace and discernment to know and appreciate the many—and sometimes, yes, mysterious— ways you work in my life for my good.

JESUS HEALS AND ASSUMES OUR BURDENS

*That evening…he cast out the spirits with a word and cured all
who were sick. This was to fulfill what had been spoken through
the prophet Isaiah, "He took our infirmities and bore our diseases."* MATTHEW 8:16, 17

U ntil they truly understood him to be the Messiah, it must
have been difficult for Jesus' followers to understand how
he had such power to heal. The writer of Mark's gospel,
thought to be the earliest gospel, calls Jesus' miracles "deeds
of power," roughly translated. At first, the disciples knew Jesus only as
a man, and though they considered him a powerful prophet, they knew
that even Isaiah and Jeremiah had not healed like this. Nor had their
revered ancestors Abraham, Moses, or David. How then did Jesus do it?
they must have wondered.

We know. He took it all on himself.

The sickness, the mental illness, the paralysis, the evil, the sin, the
grief. Each time Jesus removed one of these burdens from another, he
took them on himself. It was not the heavy wooden cross that was his
greatest burden on the path to Golgotha; it was the weight of all that
human malaise. How easy it would have been, especially after falling the
third time, to just lie there and die on the ground under the weight of it
all. I often wonder why he didn't. He had already suffered a brutal, bloody
beating, and if he'd died on the road, he could have still been buried and
raised on the third day, so why not spare himself the next six hours of
suffering?

I think it is because when we contemplate the cross, or see a repre-
sentation of one, he wanted us to see two things: that he was willing to
endure extreme suffering to purge our burdens, and that we could be
comforted by seeing a little of ourselves up there with him.

SUNDAY ▓ *Pray:* Suffering Jesus! How I wish that you had not had to carry my burdens! And how glad I am that you did!

MONDAY ▓ *Act:* Imagine your burdens—illnesses, sins, sorrows—each as a rock, small or large depending upon the burden's size. Load them into a backpack. Carry it to the foot of the empty cross where Jesus hung. Unload the backpack, naming each burden as you place a rock by the cross. Feel awed. Pick up your empty backpack and try to keep it that way.

TUESDAY ▓ *Pray:* Lord, help me release my sicknesses and sins to you, knowing that you will never suffer again because of them and that you don't want me to suffer with them.

WEDNESDAY ▓ *Act:* Write to God, describing your heaviest burden and how it hurts, what it looks like, and how it holds you back. When you finish, make the letter an offering to God. Burn it in a fireplace, bury it, or throw it into a river or stream. Release it to the earth and the elements that God created.

THURSDAY ▓ *Pray:* Selfless Master, give me the grace to shed anything in me that hurts you.

FRIDAY ▓ *Act:* A sign of your own wellness is your willingness to help another. Ease someone's burdens. You may not be able to take away sickness or sin, but you can do laundry, run errands, take him or her to church, grocery shop. Take up a sliver of Jesus' cross.

SATURDAY ▓ *Pray:* Lord, let me be an instrument of your work by teaching me to carry another's burdens.

THE LORD TAKES NOTE

But you do see! Indeed you note trouble and grief, that you may take it into your hands; the helpless commit themselves to you; you have been the helper of the orphan. **PSALM 10:14**

There are times when we feel, despite our faith and hope, that God does not see or understand what we're going through. We fear that God is far away and even farther removed from the puny course of human events. Maybe we tell ourselves that God has given up on us and can't be bothered anymore.

We are wrong and at some level know it, but we are also human. And in dire straits we can find it hard to remember that God is always near, always aware. These very human feelings are never better expressed than in the psalms, many of which, like this one, depict the wide swings of emotion, fear and faith, we all experience as humans.

The helpless commit themselves to you, writes the psalmist, and we feel this truth in our own lives. When there seems nowhere to turn, we remember that there is God to turn to. He's always been there, but in the midst of our anguish and racing hearts we just forgot. Not only has he always been there, he's there most powerfully when we realize he is all that is there, our only hope, all that stands between us and the abyss of despair.

My friend and colleague, Marion Bond West, wrote a beautiful book called *The Nevertheless Principle*, about the illness and death of her first husband. She focused on the idea of the psalmist: that when we are most in need, God is most indeed. As her title suggests, in the midst of our wrenching anxiety and desperation, God is nevertheless present: never the less, and always the more. Yup, that's God, all right.

SUNDAY ▦ *Pray:* Ever-present God, I praise you for your vigilance and protection, even when I don't recognize them.

MONDAY ▦ *Act:* Read portions of the Book of Psalms. Copy a few that "speak" to you and your situation. Carry them with you, and when you feel that you have slipped away from God, read them, remembering that he will never slip away from you.

TUESDAY ▦ *Pray:* Almighty God, protector of orphans and the sick and despised, let me lift my face to you in hope and humility.

WEDNESDAY ▦ *Act:* Reconsider your last crisis. How were you thinking of God at that time? Were you thinking of God? Did you feel abandoned? Or did God not even enter your mind? Try to see how God was present in that crisis, even if you weren't aware.

THURSDAY ▦ *Pray:* Lord, forgive me for those times when, in my human weakness, I forget that you are right beside me, ready to surround me with your loving presence.

FRIDAY ▦ *Act:* Reach out to someone who is beside herself or himself with fear and trouble, and has forgotten God without really knowing it. Remind this person of God's presence. Demonstrate God's love through prayer, psalms, practical help, and advice.

SATURDAY ▦ *Pray:* Father, I pray for those in the world whose suffering dwarfs mine, those living in the midst of violence, epidemics, desperate poverty, brutal repression. Lord, let them feel your presence.

Week Twenty

WHO IS SICK?

The Pharisees...said to his disciples, "Why does your teacher eat with tax collectors and sinners?" But Jesus said, "Those who are well have no need of a physician, but those who are sick. Go and learn what this means, 'I desire mercy, not sacrifice.'"
MATTHEW 9:11–13

We find it easy to judge between sickness and health. We know when we are well and strong; we know when we feel lousy. And we certainly know when others are well and when they are ill. It's obvious, right?

Maybe not. Who are the sick ones in this gospel passage? And do they know that they are ill? The sinners and tax collectors realize they are in need of healing. Perhaps even subconsciously, without really knowing why, they are drawn to Jesus. They seek him out, and in so doing, seek healing. And just by eating with Jesus, just by hanging out with him, their healing occurs.

The Pharisees, on the other hand, judge themselves to be perfectly well. In fact, they are so confident in that judgment that they feel free and entitled to judge the "wellness" of others. And their judgment is that the sinners and tax collectors are lacking.

They are utterly wrong, because when one has Jesus, one lacks nothing. The tax collectors and sinners have Jesus. These critical and judgmental Pharisees have laws and rules and their smug sense of self-satisfaction, all of which hide the empty sickness inside them. Jesus tries to tell them that their rules, tithes, sacrifices—all prescribed by Mosaic law—will avail them nothing without mercy.

Jesus is merciful. He has been merciful to the sinners and tax collectors, and he would be merciful to the Pharisees, if only they knew to turn to him without judgment and with mercy for others in their hearts.

SUNDAY ▪ *Pray:* Jesus, teach me to come to you, free of judgment about myself and willing to show mercy.

MONDAY ▪ *Act:* I once saw a T-shirt that said: "Hang out with Jesus. He hung for you." Today, show that you belong to Jesus. Wear a cross or a church- or faith-based T-shirt or sweatshirt, and greet everyone with "God bless you!" Don't worry about how you will be judged.

TUESDAY ▪ *Pray:* Lord, have mercy upon me in my state of sin, sickness, fear, and uncertainty! Eat with me! Talk to me! Heal me! Let me "hang out" with you.

WEDNESDAY ▪ *Act:* Are there people you've judged to be "wrong" about Jesus; people you've imagined would not be invited to hang out with him? Consider whether you've been wrong, not only by judging but in how you've judged. Because a person does not attend your church, have you decided that he or she doesn't know Jesus? Because some persons dress in a way you deem inappropriate, have you judged them unworthy of Jesus or church? Sacrifice your pride; be merciful and stop judging.

THURSDAY ▪ *Pray:* Jesus, teach me to never judge others who come to your table. Let me simply rejoice in my own invitation.

FRIDAY ▪ *Act:* Call or visit someone whom you judge to be difficult and complaining. Be merciful; don't expect him or her to change or sacrifice a need to speak of his or her trouble or dis-ease. Be compassionate. Listen as you think Jesus is listening.

SATURDAY ▪ *Pray:* Lord, when I judge myself to be well and free from sin, help me to never forget how much I need you.

Week Twenty-One

FORGIVENESS AND HEALING; HEALING AND FORGIVENESS

For your name's sake, O LORD, pardon my guilt, for it is great.
Turn to me and be gracious to me, for I am lonely and afflicted.
Relieve the troubles of my heart, and bring me out of my distress.
PSALM 25:11, 16–17

W hat is the difference between healing and forgiveness? Which comes first? Can we have one without the other? Can we have either without acknowledging our need for God to give us both?

I occasionally call a prayer line run by Silent Unity. When the prayer partner answers and asks, "How may we pray with you?" I almost always have the same response: "I want to pray for God's perfect healing and forgiveness." Sometimes the person seems a bit taken aback; they are accustomed to prayers for healing, but forgiveness? That's a bit tougher, especially when I yoke it to healing.

But I do yoke it to healing, and so, I think, does the Lord. Several times in the gospels, we witness Jesus forgiving the sins of someone who comes to him for healing, help, or protection. Sin and sickness are two sides to the same coin, and both can be fully healed only by God.

Medical science tells us regularly that excessive, negative stress can cause or worsen physical illness, and there's nothing more excessively and negatively stressful than unaddressed sin. We are, like the psalmist, burdened and afflicted by our own sins, and we are disturbed when we carry grudges or anger toward someone who has sinned against us.

Sin can be like dripping water on a stone; eventually it wears us down, erodes our soul, and makes us unwell. It is as legitimate and necessary that we turn to God to be healed from our sins as it is to seek his healing for physical sickness, especially when they have been merged.

44

SUNDAY ▨ *Pray:* Merciful Father, like the psalmist, I am burdened and afflicted by how I have offended you; I humbly and sincerely ask your forgiveness.

MONDAY ▨ *Act:* Part I: After asking for God's help and guidance, seek forgiveness from someone you've hurt. Do this personally, or call or write. Describe how your sin has both hurt him or her and burdened you. Ask for forgiveness so you both can heal.

TUESDAY ▨ *Pray:* Lord, the things I have done—or left undone—that have hurt others sicken me. Only you can heal me from this dis-ease, Lord, and I beg for this healing.

WEDNESDAY ▨ *Act:* Part II: Asking for God's help and guidance, forgive someone who has hurt you. Again, make this as personal an encounter as possible, and carry no animosity into the conversation. Grudging forgiveness is not forgiveness at all, and it will not help either of you.

THURSDAY ▨ *Pray:* Jesus, you healed by forgiving sins; teach me to recognize when sin is making me ill and to then seek the wholeness that comes with your healing pardon.

FRIDAY ▨ *Act:* Make a confession. If not to a priest or minister, confess to a faithful friend, therapist, spiritual advisor, or mentor; if you are more comfortable, go directly to God.

SATURDAY ▨ *Pray:* Lord, help me release any pain and anger against those who have hurt me, thus participating in your gifts of healing and forgiveness.

FAITH BEYOND REASON

A woman who had been suffering from hemorrhages came up behind him and touched the fringe of his cloak, for she said to herself, "If I only touch his cloak, I will be made well." Jesus turned, and seeing her he said, "Take heart, daughter, your faith has made you well." MATTHEW 9:20–22

The woman with the hemorrhage always inspires me. We learn in gospel accounts that she had suffered for many years, spending everything she had on physicians. She would have felt as an outcast. Women who bled, much less hemorrhaged, were considered ritually unclean under Mosaic law, and this would restrict considerably a woman's usual life. She undoubedly felt "shame" for this illness that had lasted for so many years.

Who knows how far she traveled to find Jesus? Or how she heard about him? Or how much pain and embarrassment it caused her to seek him? There is no indication that anyone helped her or any companion supported her. Because she had spent all her money on doctors, we know that she had nothing to spend in this quest to find Jesus.

Finally, when she finds him, she doesn't dare approach directly. She doesn't even lift her face to his. She simply tells herself that the mere touch of his clothing will heal her.

There is no ego, no self-regard. This is not rational. It is not based on anything worldly, scientific, or medically sound. It is faith beyond reason. And it works.

The most dramatic of the gospel healings—the ones we remember year after year—are the ones where those who are healed demonstrate such faith beyond reason in seeking Jesus. They are the ones who do the most, sacrifice the most, work the hardest, to reach Jesus.

"Take heart, daughter; your faith has made you well."

SUNDAY ▨ *Pray:* Lord, remove all obstacles between me and you, especially those that are in my mind.

MONDAY ▨ *Act:* Ask yourself what keeps you from acting with "faith beyond reason," what keeps you from approaching Jesus. Is it ego? Is it a "grudge" against God? Is it that you don't have the time to find him and "touch his clothing"? Is it a singular focus on medicine and science? Be honest and address these issues so that you can begin your journey to Jesus.

TUESDAY ▨ *Pray:* Jesus, give me the courage to demonstrate "faith beyond reason" when I seek your healing.

WEDNESDAY ▨ *Act:* Remind yourself that God is working through your medical professionals, whether they know it or not, and that all the good they do is from God. With that in mind at your next encounter, offer a handshake; place your hand gently on a sleeve or arm; make compassionate eye contact. Do your part to bring God into the encounter.

THURSDAY ▨ *Pray:* Great Physician, as I pursue medical intervention, remind me that you work through all medicine and all science to make us all well.

FRIDAY ▨ *Act:* Help someone who, like the hemorrhaging woman, is facing great challenges in trying to reach Jesus. Offer prayer, rides to church or medical appointments, Scripture readings, conversation, and respite from those things in that person's life that keep them from God.

SATURDAY ▨ *Pray:* Jesus, please don't let my fear and disappointment prevent me from seeking your help with a single-minded spirit.

HEALING FROM SIN

Create in me a clean heart, O God, and put a new and right spirit within me. Do not cast me away from your presence, and do not take your holy spirit from me. Restore to me the joy of your salvation, and sustain in me a willing spirit.
PSALM 51:10–12

I n this psalm of David, written after the prophet Nathan confronted David about sinning over Bathsheba, David is devastated, not just because he has committed the sins of adultery and, in effect, murder, but because he has lost God. David's spirit turned from God, and he feels this separation like a knife in his soul. He is weakened and unable to rule the kingdom; he cannot focus; he is literally sick at heart and ill-spirited.

Sin, unlike some physical illnesses, does not just go away. It is not like a virus, a cold, food poisoning, or a sprained ankle. It will not get better with time. In fact, with time and no effort, sin will fester like an infected boil, and even if the boil is invisible to others, the person living with it feels that every aspect of life suffers under its pain and rottenness.

David does what anyone living with a raging infection—whether of body, spirit, or both—would (should!) do: he turns to God. David knows it is God whom he has offended and from whom he has turned, and he knows that he will be healed and forgiven only when he turns back. But David does not stop at simply returning to God. He acknowledges, first, the great sin-sickness that he has brought upon himself; second, how he has lost God; and, third, that he is helpless to help himself. David needs God to give him a new, clean heart and a new, healthy spirit.

Are we any different?

SUNDAY ▪ *Pray:* Lord, sin-sickness has made me turn from you. Give me courage to turn back now before I become more ill-spirited.

MONDAY ▪ *Act:* Be conscious of how sin feels. How does it feel to separate yourself from God? Do you feel ill? Tired? Anxious? Accident-prone? Easily angered? Do you have indigestion? Aches and pains? Lay these "sin-sicknesses" before God as the first step in acknowledging your loss.

TUESDAY ▪ *Pray:* Kind Father, I have hurt others and I beg your forgiveness. Please undo the damage I have done and heal those I have hurt.

WEDNESDAY ▪ *Act:* David's anguish was probably intensified because he could not repair the damage: Uriah was dead. Have you sinned against someone who could be taken from you before you repent and repair? Is the person elderly, ill, depressed, or geographically distant? Don't waste time. Ask God now for a clean heart and spirit before it's too late.

THURSDAY ▪ *Pray:* Lord, the very real pain of my sin is upon me! I am in anguish for the need of the Holy Spirit. Do not treat me as I deserve, but have mercy and restore me to yourself.

FRIDAY ▪ *Act:* King David lost his way. Pray for today's leaders, that God grant them grace to use their worldly power for God and to find their way back to him when they don't.

SATURDAY ▪ *Pray:* God, as I return to you and seek healing and forgiveness, teach me to protect from future sin the clean heart and new spirit you grant me.

HAVING FAITH IN YOUR FAITH

The blind men came to him; and Jesus said to them, "Do you believe that I am able to do this?" They said, "Yes, Lord." Then he touched their eyes and said, "According to your faith let it be done to you."
MATTHEW 9:28–29

How many of us, in the position of the blind men, would have frozen in abject terror when Jesus, instead of simply restoring our sight, said to us, "According to your faith, let it be done to you"?

The first part of their appeal is easy. Who wouldn't go to Jesus, if given such an amazing opportunity, to be healed? Who wouldn't jump at the chance to bring the thing that has been making us miserable, ruining our lives, causing us pain...and hand it over to Jesus, miracle-worker, healer, Son of God?

We'd be overjoyed! We'd rush to him, fall on our knees, and then anticipate the blessed relief that would come when he took away our overwhelming nightmare and gave us the dream of life again. And we wouldn't stop to think, at first, why he was asking us something so obvious. Do we believe? Of course we believe! Why would we be here otherwise? Now, let's get to it, Lord; we've been waiting a long time.

He touches the broken part of us. We can almost feel it starting! We tremble with anticipation! Good life...here we come!

We know he can do it...right? Of course he can! He's Jesus! So what if he looks, well, sort of normal? He's better than all the doctors...isn't he? He does think I'm worth it...doesn't he?

"According to your faith, let it be done to you."

SUNDAY ▪ *Pray:* Jesus, my body and spirit are not strong enough for the kind of faith I want to have! Where I am weak, Lord, be strong for me!

MONDAY ▪ *Act:*
1: Make a list of every good thing in your life that comes from God.
2: Read your list.
3: If it doesn't contain every good thing in your life...see number 1.

TUESDAY ▪ *Pray:* Lord, help me to remember that every time I open my eyes and see, you work the same miracle for me that you did for the blind men.

WEDNESDAY ▪ *Act:* Faith is like the muscle that is your heart. It gets stronger with work. Practice faith. I don't think many humans possess the kind of faith that completely banishes fear, but today, select one small thing that causes you fear. Give it to God. Every time your mind returns to it, remember how the blind men answered Jesus and say, "Yes, Lord, I believe you can take this from me."

THURSDAY ▪ *Pray:* Compassionate Jesus, I have faith in you, even when I don't have faith in myself.

FRIDAY ▪ *Act:* Write to God, detailing the ways in which your faith is weak. Ask for his forgiveness and, just as important, for the grace that will carry you beyond human limitations to a deeper faith.

SATURDAY ▪ *Pray:* Lord, I want so badly to have the faith of the blind men! Let me discern the ways in which you lead me to a stronger faith.

Week Twenty-Five

OVERWHELMED WITH PAIN
AND SUFFERING

---

*Hear my prayer, O Lord, let my cry come to you. For my days
pass away like smoke, and my bones burn like a furnace. My
heart is stricken and withered like grass; I am too wasted to eat
my bread. Because of my loud groaning my bones cling to my skin.*
Psalm 102:1, 3–5

T here are times when illness is so debilitating, so exhausting and
painful, that we can hardly pray, or even know how. We don't
have the energy, and sometimes we don't have much hope. We
are not sure that God is listening, because (we tell ourselves) if
he was listening, how is it that we continue to suffer?

That kind of illness reduces us to the blind, uncomprehending, undis-
cerning, needful state of infancy. We no longer know what is wrong or
why or how it went wrong; we just know that we want relief, and we don't
know why we aren't getting it.

But we are not infants. Even in our most dire suffering, we are the
grown children of God. We know the wonder of the world he has created
and the wonder of those we love whom he has created. We have experienced his goodness, plenitude, and omnipotence. We may not feel these
things now, but we have been the beneficiaries of them at some point.
They are lodged in our consciousness, and if we can't feel that they are
there, we can choose to know and remember that they happened.

We have access to God.

Like the psalmist, we can cry, even wordlessly, to God. We can ask God
to hear us, knowing that he always does. We can ask him to remember us,
knowing that he never forgets us. We can ask him to stay with us through
this pain, knowing he has never left.

SUNDAY ▨ *Pray:* Beloved God, hear my cry of agony; help me to know in every fiber of my being that you do hear me, that you are with me.

MONDAY ▨ *Act:* Reach beyond your pain to the hand of God. Envision this. Lift your hand toward God; if you are not able, lift your hand in spirit. Feel God's gentle grasp, not just of your hand but of your entire self. Relax into his cradling hands and arms.

TUESDAY ▨ *Pray:* Lord, please bring me relief and help me wait in the humming peace of your presence until this too shall pass from me.

WEDNESDAY ▨ *Act:* Rest in God. Literally allow yourself to sleep; or if you can't sleep, lie still. Understand that you are in God's shadow. Let yourself be there and stay there. Remember that pain changes and will eventually end, but God will never end and doesn't change.

THURSDAY ▨ *Pray:* Father, let me rest in the knowledge that you never abandon me.

FRIDAY ▨ *Act:* Make sure there is a crucifix visible to you, or keep the image of Christ crucified in your mind. When pain and suffering overwhelm you, fix your eyes—or your mind's eye—on this image. Ask Jesus to allow you to share in his suffering.

SATURDAY ▨ *Pray:* Lord, let me remember that when all the layers of pain and life itself are stripped away, you remain with me, in me.

WHEN BAD THINGS HAPPEN...

Then Job answered the LORD: *"I know that you can do all things, and that no purpose of yours can be thwarted. Therefore I have uttered what I did not understand, things too wonderful for me, which I did not know. I had heard of you by the hearing of the ear, but now my eye sees you."* JOB 42:1–2, 3, 5

Job's story is the one we all dread. How does a good man, a godly man, come to such a pass? Why do we—who try to do everything right, to follow God and do good—suffer? It's that aggravating question: Why do bad things happen to good people...especially when we are the "good people"?

No matter what anyone says, only God knows the answer. What Job eventually learns after blaming fate, others, and even God, is that he can't begin to fathom God or plumb the depths of his mind and majesty.

Neither can we.

When ill and troubled, we all feel like Job: anxious, vulnerable, wondering why we must suffer. What have we done wrong? Like Job, we may even question God. But when God responds with some of Scripture's most striking passages describing his omnipotence and immeasurable power, Job experiences a revelation that is helpful to us: it is through suffering that Job comes to know God better. Job moves closer to God through his afflictions.

At first, Job does what many of us might be inclined to do. He turns away from God, seeking worldly advice and feeling sorry for himself. It is only when Job seeks God that he receives a measure of peace. Job is healed twice by God: first, through the peace that comes in accepting God's power, and, second, in physical and personal healing.

None of us want to experience Job's travails. But it is comforting to know that Job's way is open to us. He uses his pain to seek God. And God heals him.

SUNDAY ▨ *Pray:* Great God, when I suffer, instead of asking, "Why?" let me ask, "How can I use my pain to grow closer to you?"

MONDAY ▨ *Act:* Observe God's greatness. Take notice of all that God has wrought. Everything you see has been created by God and given to us. Imagine such generosity! Remind yourself that God is waiting for you to absorb his generosity.

TUESDAY ▨ *Pray:* Lord, as I see those around me living their healthy lives, remind me that even if my life is different now, your presence in my life never changes.

WEDNESDAY ▨ *Act:* Let God's great generosity work through you by buying or making a gift for someone in need of healing. If you are housebound, shop online or over the phone. If you have no money, make something; a homemade card will do. Feel God's grace moving through you.

THURSDAY ▨ *Pray:* Jesus, when I am afraid, help me turn to you and remember that, in love, you suffered for me and for all. You did not let fear stand between you and me.

FRIDAY ▨ *Act:* Give up something you like today: a food, a television program, music. Make the sacrifice deliberately to make room for God and his healing power within you.

SATURDAY ▨ *Pray:* Mary, Mother of God, you suffered willingly, accepting doubts about your miraculous pregnancy, childbirth far from home, the sword piercing your heart. Teach me to turn where you turned: to God.

NO TIME FOR THE HEALER TO HEAL

Now when Jesus heard (about John the Baptist's execution), he withdrew...to a deserted place by himself. But when the crowds heard it, they followed...and he had compassion on them and cured their sick. MATTHEW 14:13, 14

J esus has just learned that his cousin, the one who knew him from the womb and leapt for joy, had been beheaded by Herod. John the Baptist, who declared Jesus the Messiah and Son of God, had been killed by the same king who would soon help condemn Jesus to death.

Jesus, subject to the same sorrows and pains as any person, is heartsick and grieving. He wants—needs—to be somewhere quiet, alone, where he can mourn and prepare himself for what is coming, for he alone knows what John's death portends for his own future. Jesus needs time alone with God.

He doesn't get it, though, because the crowds—also roiled by John's execution and confused about what it means—are desperate to be with Jesus, the one left to them, the healer. They don't care about Jesus' need for solitude or, truthfully, about his needs at all.

Do we ever really think about what God needs when we need him?

Jesus, in the deserted place where he has chosen to mourn and commune with the Father, sees the people coming from every direction. He must have wanted, with every part of his human being, to send them away, to shout, "Can't you see that I need this time? Can't you give me just this little thing?"

But Jesus knows they can't. He takes a deep breath, draws upon his compassion...and begins to cure them.

SUNDAY ▧ *Pray:* Jesus, my need for you is deep and instinctive, even selfish. Have compassion on me, Lord!

MONDAY ▧ *Act:* Have empathy for Jesus. Consider that he experienced the same feelings as you do. Imagine his disappointment at being misunderstood, his anger at the disrespect shown to the Father, his exhaustion after traveling for miles upon miles, his hunger when there was no food, his agony at the flogging, his shuddering, painful breaths on the cross.

TUESDAY ▧ *Pray:* Lord, teach me to have compassion for you, as you look upon the world you created.

WEDNESDAY ▧ *Act:* Have empathy for God, the Father. Consider his sorrow for how we have treated his gift of the natural world, his dismay at wars, especially those waged by those falsely invoking his name, his disgust that some of his children starve in a world of plenty, his anger and disappointment at injustice and racism.

THURSDAY ▧ *Pray:* Jesus, when I am heartsick, remind me that you, while on earth, experienced the same pain and suffering.

FRIDAY ▧ *Act:* Have empathy for the Holy Spirit. Consider how the Spirit hovers, waiting to be welcomed into our lives, and imagine his sadness at our closed hearts, his horror at the damage we do in disregarding his wisdom, his pain when we welcome God with our lips only, his hurt at being ignored.

SATURDAY ▧ *Pray:* Lord, in my fear and longing, I am among the crowds, running blindly to you in hope and need. Comfort me, Lord!

COURAGE ONLY IN GOD

Their courage melted away in their calamity; they reeled and staggered like drunkards, and were at their wits' end. Then they cried to the LORD in their trouble, and he brought them out from their distress; he made the storm be still, and the waves of the sea were hushed. PSALM 107:26–29

W e like to think of ourselves as capable, even proficient and independent. We like to hear ourselves described as "tough," "strong," "clever," "successful." Our hearts leap proudly when someone says, "She's really at the top of her game," or "He knows what he's doing; I wouldn't want to mess with him."

Such descriptions make us feel just a little invincible, a little ahead of the poor "other guy" who's not quite as successful, maybe even a little more blessed than the average person. We are confident, maybe a little full of ourselves, even a little forgetful of God in our lives.

But then something happens. We get sick. We lose a loved one. We get a new supervisor who isn't so enamored of us. We disappoint someone. We feel anxious, depressed, or sick with grief.

What then? Like those described by the psalmist, we go running for God! Our little castle, built mostly in our minds, has collapsed, and we want help! We are at our wits' end; we do feel calamity; we reel around not knowing what to do. And we call upon the Lord, suddenly remembering that only in God can we find real courage and true security. Only God is truly capable, tough, strong, clever, successful. Only God can rescue us from our distress, calm our storms, and heal our ills.

SUNDAY ▓ *Pray:* Lord, I fall to my knees before you in humility and gratitude, before I am driven to my knees in fear and pain.

MONDAY ▓ *Act:* List the five things you are most proud of in your life. Would you have achieved any of these things without God? Humbly thank God for each one of them and ask him to continue to intervene for the good in your life.

TUESDAY ▓ *Pray:* Father, I praise you for every single positive event and achievement in my life, for without you I am nothing, have nothing, can be nothing.

WEDNESDAY ▓ *Act:* Consider a past crisis in your life and how it was resolved. Think about all the ways that God intervened, calming storms, healing brokenness. Write down every way in which God helped. When you next feel disturbed and ill, return to this list. Return to God.

THURSDAY ▓ *Pray:* Understanding God, just as I turn to you as a supplicant in need, remind me to offer you thanksgiving when life goes well.

FRIDAY ▓ *Act:* Act as God's agent for someone who is in a life crisis. Do whatever God gives you to do to help still the storm and hush the waves in his or her life. Remembering that God acts in every aspect of our lives, offer personal, practical, spiritual, and prayerful help.

SATURDAY ▓ *Pray:* Lord, my body, mind, and spirit are in upheaval. Please calm the storms and dis-ease within me.

COME FORWARD

He said to the man who had the withered hand, "Come forward."
Then he said to them, "Is it lawful to do good or...harm on the sab-
bath, to save a life or to destroy it?" But they were silent. He looked
around at them with anger; he was grieved at their hardness of
heart and said to the man, "Stretch out your hand." He stretched
it out and his hand was restored. **MARK 3:3–5**

C an our illness help others? Does God have a purpose for our suffering, and even our humiliation, that we don't immediately comprehend?

Who can know the mind and plan of God?

We can, however, be guided by Jesus, and there are certainly healing miracles where he seems to act as much for the witnesses as for the healed. Here, not only does Jesus call the maimed man to the front of the synagogue, which had to be somewhat humiliating for someone who already was likely considered "half" a man, but the Lord then uses him as an object lesson. Jesus is intent on healing the man but also on demonstrating that Sabbath laws must be flexible enough to allow for God's good work.

Jesus is not really trying to reach the Pharisees and scribes; he already knows how they will react, though he is angry and disappointed in them. His real target audience is probably the others in the synagogue, those "on the fence," who may be moved in the direction of good. It is for these that Jesus restores the man, as much as for the man himself. The maimed man is not the only one healed by what happens. The witnesses are offered an opportunity to be healed as well.

Are illnesses God's opportunities for us to "model" faith? Do we have the courage to follow the man with the withered hand and step forward to demonstrate faith in God?

SUNDAY ▨ *Pray:* Jesus, help me to see beyond my own pain to discern my role in your plan.

MONDAY ▨ *Act:* Respond to God's call to model faith through your own illness or trouble. Is this situation an opportunity to become less judgmental? Can you learn to become more empathetic to others facing difficult challenges? Are you more able to discern when another is "hiding" his or her pain?

TUESDAY ▨ *Pray:* Lord, give me the courage to be used by you to help others increase their faith.

WEDNESDAY ▨ *Act:* Write a letter to the editor or contribute to an online blog or forum on your illness. Explain what you live with, but more importantly, how others can be helpful and respectful to people like you. Talk about your faith in God's plan, and urge readers to be compassionate.

THURSDAY ▨ *Pray:* Jesus, teach me to walk on the faithful side of the line between displaying my illness and demonstrating my belief in your healing power.

FRIDAY ▨ *Act:* Think of someone you have dismissed or even disdained because of their appearance or behavior. Could that person have been acting out of pain or dis-ease? Might she or he have been experiencing distress or illness and trying to hide it? Reach out to this person. If she or he is no longer accessible to you, ask God's forgiveness and reach out to the next person you meet in a similar situation.

SATURDAY ▨ *Pray:* Merciful Lord, let me never feel embarrassed to answer your call to healing or action.

HONEST, STEADFAST, SAVING GOD

For you have delivered my soul from death, my eyes from tears, my feet from stumbling. I walk before the Lord in the land of the living. I kept my faith, even when I said, "I am greatly afflicted"; I said in my consternation, "Everyone is a liar." **PSALM 116:8–11**

W hen we are sick, sick at heart, or ill-spirited, we can say things we regret. We may even know as we say them that they are not good, not appropriate, not godly. But our dis-ease gets the better of us, or we give it the better of us, and off we fly, mouths running. Sadly, it is often those closest to us who bear the brunt of our pain-driven words. Our spouses, children, caretakers, nurses, doctors, even our older parents, can become targets of our hurt and anger.

It's hard in the midst of confusion and illness not to want to "take it out" on someone, or just plain get it out of us. We are too filled with angst and pain; we have to get rid of it. We complain bitterly (I am greatly afflicted); we lash out (Everyone is a liar).

Underneath all this very human (read: flawed) behavior beats a steady, comforting truth: we still have faith. We know we are sick and behaving badly as a result, but we also know that we are not lost before the Lord. We keep our faith! And that faith allows us, eventually, to calm down, to feel better, to know that God will heal us and, as importantly, forgive our frustrations and outbursts.

We also know that we can ask forgiveness of those we hurt with our pain. This is one way we can set our world right as God delivers us.

SUNDAY ▦ *Pray:* God of deliverance, free me from the chaos and pain that have engulfed me, and let me feel your peace settle around me.

MONDAY ▦ *Act:* Remember the last time you snapped at someone because you were ill or hurt. God has delivered you from that painful moment, and now you have the opportunity to apologize to the person you hurt. Do it.

TUESDAY ▦ *Pray:* Lord, even when I feel that everyone has let me down and that I have let myself down, I know that you will never let me down.

WEDNESDAY ▦ *Act:* When you find yourself about to speak sharply to someone because you are ill, tired, confused, or distressed, stop yourself. Tell the person, "I am really feeling crummy, and I was about to say something mean. I'm choosing not to because you don't deserve that. Thanks for being here." And then see where that opening leads.

THURSDAY ▦ *Pray:* Father, forgive me for those times when I have hurt others in my dis-ease. Keep me from lashing out.

FRIDAY ▦ *Act:* Think about the last time someone spoke harshly to you. Even if you don't know what was wrong, you can be sure that something was hurting her or him. The next time it happens, with that person or anyone, don't snap back. Instead, tell the person you understand that they are feeling badly, and ask how you can help. Or simply remain supportively silent.

SATURDAY ▦ *Pray:* Good God, thank you for understanding!

HUMBLE STATE OF PREPAREDNESS

O LORD, my heart is not lifted up, my eyes are not raised too high; I do not occupy myself with things too great and too marvelous for me. But I have calmed and quieted my soul.
PSALM 131:1–2

From the humility of these words, it is difficult to believe that the writer was one of the most powerful and renowned kings in history. This psalm of David reads as though the king is in the perfect, humble state of preparation, waiting for God's healing and help.

We hear so much today about "preparedness." Homeland Security is prepared for a terrorist attack. With global warming, we are advised to prepare for violent weather and possible power outages. We buy generators, batteries, and candles, and stock our pantries as we watch CNN and the Weather Channel. We carry cell phones closer to our bodies than wallets, lest we miss an alert or message. We want to be prepared for anything.

Are we any less anxious or healthy for all this preparedness?

Are we prepared for God?

Millennia ago, David had already learned something we are still trying to grasp. The only way to be truly prepared is to humbly and confidently wait on the Lord. Can we be humble and confident at the same time? Of course: we are humble because we know human preparedness can avail us nothing without God, and we are confident in God, the only power able to heal and save us.

That serenity that David expresses—that peace that surpasses all understanding—simply can't be gotten with technology or hyper-awareness. It can only be found in God...then, now, and always.

SUNDAY ▧ *Pray:* Lord, when my heart is lifted too high in pride at my knowledge and preparedness, gently remind me to lower my eyes before your mighty power.

MONDAY ▧ *Act:* Become unprepared. Follow David's counsel and lower your eyes from the frenzy of an uncertain world. Don't read or watch the news. Don't go online. Turn off the television. Spend time "preparing" with the Lord in the quiet of your soul.

TUESDAY ▧ *Pray:* Father, teach me that the only preparing I need to do is to ready myself for your words, healing, and forgiveness.

WEDNESDAY ▧ *Act:* Consider a time in your life when you drove yourself crazy "preparing," only to have things go wrong—or go "different"—despite your plans and preparations. What did you gain or learn from that time?

THURSDAY ▧ *Pray:* Loving God, as I prepare myself in practical ways for the storms of this world, keep me close within the ark of your love where there is true safety.

FRIDAY ▧ *Act:* Concentrate on the following phrase: "Man prepares; God repairs." Repeat it whenever you feel anxious or pressed to prepare for a prospective illness or calamity.

SATURDAY ▧ *Pray:* Lord, teach me to find your healing presence within the quiet you have placed in my heart.

A CRUSHING LOVE

He told the disciples to have a boat ready for him because of the crowd, so that they would not crush him; for he had cured many, so that all who had diseases pressed upon him to touch him.
MARK 3:9–10

For most people, it would have been like a scene from a horror movie: the mob, realizing that healing and relief flowed from the touch, the very clothing, of Jesus, become frenzied in their need. They press forward—blind, maimed, drooling, bruised, bleeding, covered with sores and scabs, dressed in rags, stinking, muttering and screeching in the grip of mental illness—each desperate to touch him. Some of them no longer see Jesus as a person. His needs, his fears, his human desire to draw back repulsed—these mean nothing to them. For some in the mob, Jesus is a mere means to an end.

His back is to the water. There is nowhere for him to go; he will either be mobbed or drowned. Exhausted from healing and helping this mob for hours, Jesus shouts to the disciples to get a boat ready. He climbs into it, but still they come because they need what he has for them, and he cannot turn them away.

The truth is hard for us to admit: Jesus' love for us crushed him. We are that mob. We want so much, need so much, especially healing and forgiveness. If Jesus never turned away from us then, despite aching bones, exhaustion, and his human nature, we can be sure he will never turn away from us now. After all, he was willing to be crushed in our crowds and crushed on a cross.

SUNDAY ▨ *Pray:* Jesus, forgive me for the many times when my needs blind me to your sacrifices.

MONDAY ▨ *Act:* How much of your communication with God is composed of requests (demands?) for your healing or another's healing? Today, compose prayers and messages of thanks and praise and... nothing else.

TUESDAY ▨ *Pray:* Lord, I bless and praise you for your patience and strength while on earth among men and women, even as you suffered the same physical and natural limitations as the rest of us.

WEDNESDAY ▨ *Act:* Once Jesus got into the boat, some in the crowd came to their senses and realized they were blessed just to be able to sit near him. Sit quietly with Jesus today. He doesn't need to hear your needs to know you. Rest with—and in—the Lord and Messiah.

THURSDAY ▨ *Pray:* Jesus, help me to avoid crushing others with my needs and demands as I pursue healing and wholeness.

FRIDAY ▨ *Act:* Assist Jesus. Let someone in great need "crush" you with demands. Take on one task for another that is "above and beyond" your call of duty. Do it cheerfully, willingly, compassionately, and never forget that Jesus did this every minute of every day of his life...and death.

SATURDAY ▨ *Pray:* Lord, let me work to ensure that the community with which I worship never becomes a mob that sees you as one-dimensional, as only an answer to our needs.

WHY ARE YOU AFRAID?

But he was in the stern, asleep...and they woke him and said..."Teacher, do you not care that we are perishing?" He rebuked the wind, and said to the sea, "Peace! Be still!" Then the wind ceased and there was a dead calm. He said, "Why are you afraid? Have you still no faith?" **MARK 4:38–40**

There are times when I think I am going to die. And not in the distant future. Almost always these times are accompanied by searing, choking, paralytic fear. My guess is that most people who have seen a lab report with their name and the word "malignant" on the same page have had this same experience.

I'm not proud that I still occasionally feel this way, but it is something of a relief to know that I'm in good company. In one way or another, many of us know just how the apostles felt in that boat. It was a malignant storm, a stomach-churning, heart-racing, paralysis-inducing, sickening storm. If nature had prevailed, they were about to die. Some of us have or have had illnesses that—absent God's intervention through personal healing, medical science, and the brilliance of researchers and technology—might have killed us. We know how it feels to need God's intervention to calm the storm of illness and fear.

I like to think that if I'd been an apostle on that boat, I'd have known better and trusted Jesus without becoming terrified. But who am I kidding? Yes, the apostles had Jesus with them, but before he calmed the storm, they still were not sure exactly who their teacher was. Perhaps that was their excuse when he asked them, "Have you still no faith?"

What's mine? What's yours? We know precisely who Jesus is.

SUNDAY ▪ *Pray:* Jesus, forgive my fearful human nature, especially when I "know better" who you are and what you can do.

MONDAY ▪ *Act:* Share your fears. It helps to know you're not alone. Have a Fear Party. Invite people living with fear; ask everyone to share what she or he is most afraid of and how fear impacts his or her relationship with God. Also share prayers and coping strategies.

TUESDAY ▪ *Pray:* Lord, give me courage to face fear, knowing that you are my strength and my refuge.

WEDNESDAY ▪ *Act:* Close your eyes. Imagine your fear as an illness, a dis-ease, to bring before Jesus reclining in the boat. Your fears are like wind and waves, threatening to engulf you. See Jesus stand between you and the wind and waves, commanding, "Peace! Be still!" Where is your faith? Right there.

THURSDAY ▪ *Pray:* Jesus, when, like the apostles, I am about to drown in my fear, if not the Sea of Galilee, show me that fear is a storm that cannot stand in your presence.

FRIDAY ▪ *Act:* Consider your worst fear. Breathing deeply and slowly, ask yourself, "What if it happens?" With God beside you, stay calm as you confront the answer. Ask God to spare you from this, while remembering that he is there with you now and will be forever, no matter what.

SATURDAY ▪ *Pray:* Jesus, remind me that there is nothing that can happen to me, no place where I can be, where you are not already there waiting to protect me.

HIS STEADFAST LOVE

Some were sick...and endured affliction...Then they cried out to the LORD in their trouble, and he saved them from their distress; he sent out his word and healed them, and delivered them from destruction. Let them thank the LORD for his steadfast love, for his wonderful works to humankind. **PSALM 107:17, 19–21**

The psalms are filled with pleas to God for help, confessions of unworthiness, and talk of the dire state of humankind. Not so different from today, really. God always comes through for us; he never needs to be reminded of our need. His love is steadfast.

Yet, as is the case in this passage, we seem to constantly need to be reminded to thank him. How many times do we pray for little things— "Lord, please don't let this sore throat be the start of the flu"..."Jesus, don't let me be late to pick up my kid"..."Dear God, help me not to mess up this lunch with the boss"—but when our prayers are answered, we forget to thank God? In fact, we often forget that God helped us at all. Suddenly, we're all, "Wow, the vitamin C worked!"..."Good thing I hit all the green lights!"..."Did you see the look on the boss's face when I told that great joke?"

And God in his steadfast love is left standing alone with the check.

Why are we so quick to forget God's work in caring for us, in answering our prayers, small and large, even the ones we neglect to say aloud? Why do we ignore "his wonderful works to humankind," or worse, ascribe God's amazing works to our own purported skill and brilliance?

Is it so difficult to thank God because we don't like to think about how utterly we need him, how completely we depend upon him, and how much, in his steadfast love, he gives to us? After all, it's only every single breath.

SUNDAY ▩ *Pray:* Steadfast and loving Father, thank you for the food and drink I consume, the medicine I take, the place where I dwell, the shelter and sustenance I enjoy every day of my life.

MONDAY ▩ *Act:* List a few favorite foods and drinks. Consider what it takes for each item to get to you: how and where is each ingredient grown or produced? Who produces/prepares the final product? Who packages it and how? How is it transported? Where do you purchase it? Who is your cashier or waiter? Think of all that God does so you can enjoy a bite of chocolate or sip of wine.

TUESDAY ▩ *Pray:* Good God, thank you for the people I love, the people who challenge me, the people I work and worship with.

WEDNESDAY ▩ *Act:* Think of five good things that happened to you in the past week. Did you thank God for each? If not, why not? Did you forget? Did you subconsciously assume that God had nothing to do with your "luck"?

THURSDAY ▩ *Pray:* Almighty God, through whom all things exist and without whom nothing exists, let me never cease to praise and glorify you.

FRIDAY ▩ *Act:* Become part of God's production love-chain for others. Bake someone a treat. Deliver takeout. Knit a scarf. Plant a garden. Bring flowers or fresh vegetables to a neighbor.

SATURDAY ▩ *Pray:* Creator God, thank you for...everything! And especially for forgiving me when I neglect to thank you.

HE LOOKED UP TO HEAVEN

Taking the five loaves and two fish, he looked up to heaven, and blessed and broke the loaves, and gave them to his disciples to set before the people; and he divided the two fish among them all. And all ate and were filled. MARK 6:41–42

Five thousand men, plus women and children. All faint with hunger. All likely to become sick with hunger and exhaustion before reaching their distant homes on foot. The disciples are concerned and frustrated. What are they supposed to do now? They can only find a few loaves and fishes among all these people. Will they be blamed when people become weak and sick as they try to reach their homes? What if some of the older ones collapse? Will Jesus be blamed? Will this be used against him?

We know what happens next. Jesus is, in a way, putting on a performance. He is performing for the people, emphasizing that everything he has taught them is true because he can also perform the miracle of feeding them and achieving what is, in essence, a preventative healing. They will not become sick and weak from hunger. Jesus is also performing for the apostles, asking them once again, "Where is your faith?" He puts their frustration and worry to shame. He is also performing for his enemies, who will soon hear about this over-the-top miracle.

And Jesus is performing for us. This is one miracle no one forgets. It is a very public demonstration that Jesus knows and understands our physiological needs. He is God and man, and thus knows the pain of hunger and its consequences. We may forget exactly what he said to the thousands in that daylong teaching session, but we will not forget how he ended the course. He looked up to heaven, and blessed the loaves.

SUNDAY ▨ *Pray:* Lord, when I, like the apostles, fear that I don't have enough, help me to remember the loaves and fishes.

MONDAY ▨ *Act:* Host a Scripture reading and discussion at your home and break bread after or during the discussion. Say a blessing over the bread and other food and drink, asking God to multiply the blessings of his words among all of you so that you can spread these blessings.

TUESDAY ▨ *Pray:* Jesus, when I am in danger of fainting or becoming ill with hunger for you, lead me to a quiet place and time to spend with you.

WEDNESDAY ▨ *Act:* Say a blessing before every meal or snack. If you already do this in the privacy of your home, challenge yourself to ask for God's blessing over food you take with others or in a public place such as a restaurant or cafeteria.

THURSDAY ▨ *Pray:* Lord, forgive me for the times when I try to stuff the emptiness in me with food rather than with your teachings.

FRIDAY ▨ *Act:* Join or start a community garden. No earthly force can multiply food faster than a large vegetable garden, as anyone with hundreds of zucchini will testify to in August. Plan for the excess produce to be donated to a soup kitchen or food pantry.

SATURDAY ▨ *Pray:* Jesus, thank you for nourishing me with your words so that I may be strong in spirit and ready to do your will.

GOD'S SPIRIT IN ALL THINGS

But you are merciful to all, for you can do all things, and you overlook people's sins so that they may repent. You spare all things, for they are yours, O Lord, you who love the living. For your immortal spirit is in all things. **Wisdom: 11:23, 26—12:1**

Afuneral director who is a friend of mine has a theory about healing. He believes that when someone experiences what seems to be miraculous healing, the miracle may not be only in the healing but also in the second chance God provides by giving the person more time.

To do what? Depends on the person. Depends on us. My friend thinks it may be for each of us to get it right. We have all experienced healing in some form, whether the quiet, private healing of God's forgiveness, or the dramatic, obvious healing of a miraculous "cure." Why has God healed and forgiven us? Solomon assures us that it's because God loves us and wants to spare us what we might be facing if he takes us sooner rather than later. We belong to him, Solomon says, and as his, we are given another chance to make our lives right according to his Spirit within us. We belong to God, and God wants to give us every opportunity to realize that. God does not want to see his own work, in which dwells his Holy Spirit, crushed or separated from him.

My funeral friend has heard many preachers offer funeral services. One of the most memorable was for a fine young man in seemingly perfect health with a wife and young family who had died suddenly. To a packed congregation the minister said, "We are all here to ask 'Why him?' Perhaps we should ask 'Why not me?'"

SUNDAY ▦ *Pray:* Merciful God, you gave Solomon great wisdom, and yet I ask only for the wisdom to discern my small part in your plan.

MONDAY ▦ *Act:* Examine yourself. Whether you feel well or sick right now, ask yourself: Why has God given me the time I have left on this earth? What is God's immortal Spirit in me directing me to do? What parts of me do I need to build up, and what parts do I need to release?

TUESDAY ▦ *Pray:* Father, give me ears to hear your Spirit within me despite the clamor all around me.

WEDNESDAY ▦ *Act:* God is merciful to us, giving us the time we need to repent and improve if we choose to take it. Are you merciful? Have you given others the time to discern their mistakes and repent? Have you given them the time and space to come back into your life?

THURSDAY ▦ *Pray:* O God! I am weak and afraid! Give me the courage to do whatever I have left to do…for you.

FRIDAY ▦ *Act:* Prepare a "bucket list," but instead of listing the things you want to do for yourself before you die, list things you want to do for God. Then, get started, knowing that God will give you the time he decides you need.

SATURDAY ▦ *Pray:* All-knowing Lord, I praise and thank you for giving me the time I need to become more fully your child.

PATIENCE AND PRIVACY

When he had put saliva on his eyes and laid his hands upon him, he asked him, "Can you see anything?" The man...said, "I can see people, but they look like trees, walking." Then Jesus laid his hands on his eyes again; and he looked intently and his sight was restored and he saw everything clearly. **MARK 8:23–25**

What a fascinating passage from the normally taciturn Mark! It is one of the only gospel healings where Jesus deliberately draws someone far away from the ever-present, ever-watching crowd and goes through an extended process to bring about healing. We know it wasn't necessary for Jesus to do all this; we know that Jesus could have healed the blind man without a word or even a breath. We know that many had been healed from great distances or just by touching Jesus' cloak!

So what happened here? Why did Jesus draw this particular man away into a private place? And why the ritual "washing" of the blinded eyes? What did Jesus know about this man that Mark didn't or doesn't tell us? Was there a private dialogue between Jesus and the man—something necessary for the man's inner healing—that was not recorded?

As with so many of the extraordinary moments in Jesus' life, we simply can't know. Maybe Jesus wanted to make sure that the Pharisees would learn every detail of this elaborate healing and be confounded by it. Perhaps Jesus wanted to leave the memory of a deeply intimate healing imprinted on our hearts and minds.

Or maybe Jesus wanted us to realize that we don't always get healed instantly, that healing is an individual thing, that it may not be tidy, that it can take time and effort and patience. And, yes, faith.

SUNDAY ▦ *Pray:* Lord, when I am impatient and desperate for healing, remind me that you, and not I, know best what I need and when.

***

MONDAY ▦ *Act:* The health care world can seem like a minefield: slow and precarious. But God, as we see in this gospel, works in mysterious ways. Consider whether the Lord, through your healing process, is giving you an opportunity to participate in your own wellness in ways you haven't thought of.

***

TUESDAY ▦ *Pray:* Jesus, forgive me for the times when I want you to wave a healing wand and restore my life to perfection without me having to lift a finger to participate in the process.

***

WEDNESDAY ▦ *Act:* Take action, as you are able, to participate in God's healing process. Eat more healthily. Exercise and get more rest. Meditate. Attend a spiritual retreat. Do stretching and deep breathing.

***

THURSDAY ▦ *Pray:* Blessed Teacher, I thank you for teaching me that your precious healing is not a one-size-fits-all prospect.

***

FRIDAY ▦ *Act:* Read this gospel passage with someone who is struggling with the slow, frustrating pace of his or her own healing. Discuss what it means and how it can apply to her or his situation. Help him or her to discern ways to participate in God's healing plan. Encourage the person to spend quiet time with God.

***

SATURDAY ▦ *Pray:* Jesus, show me what I should do to faithfully participate in your healing of my dis-ease.

HEALING FOR GLOBAL MALAISE

They shall beat their swords into plowshares, and their spears into pruning hooks; nation shall not lift up sword against nation, neither shall they learn war any more. Isaiah 2:4

As I write this, the United States Congress is assembling to vote on whether our country should bomb Syria. As best I can understand it, the "logic" behind this push for an act of war seems to be that because the besieged and dictatorial Syrian leader has mercilessly killed some of his people, the United States should mercilessly kill some of his remaining people...to teach him a lesson about not killing his people.

So much for Isaiah's prophecy.

Except.

Isaiah prophesied a coming time of God's mercy, when he would heal the people of the sins and warlike nature that had overcome them. God would show us the way to live in peace, to heal our greed, hatred, and thirst for revenge. Jesus was the herald of that time. He offered the world—us—an alternative to war, an alternative to our bloody human inclinations. His teachings were simple and completely against what has become human nature: love others, be willing to suffer rather than to make others suffer, give rather than take, serve rather than enslave, die rather than kill.

So the time Isaiah described was indeed manifested. God did indeed keep his promise to his errant people. The healer of the world's pain and anger did indeed come and make his message clear in his teachings, life, death, and resurrection. We have the words, the example, the forgiveness, and the healing necessary to start again. God has given us everything we need to heal the world.

But will we?

SUNDAY ▩ *Pray:* God and Father, thank you for giving us chance after chance to follow the way of peace and healing you promised through Isaiah and delivered in Jesus.

MONDAY ▩ *Act:* Join or form a prayer group that focuses on manifesting peace in your community, the country, and the world.

TUESDAY ▩ *Pray:* Jesus, Son of God, we thank you for spending—and giving—your life on earth in order to teach us how to heal our world and live in peace.

WEDNESDAY ▩ *Act:* Contribute time and money to a group that either works for peace or helps refugees of war and violence. Some include Catholic Charities, Episcopal Relief, Care, Americares, International Catholic Migration Commission, Doctors without Borders, Friends Committee on National Legislation, Lutheran Immigration and Refugee Service, Unicef, and the Red Cross.

THURSDAY ▩ *Pray:* Wise Holy Spirit, thank you for coming among us to guide us on the path to global community and healing cooperation.

FRIDAY ▩ *Act:* Examine your life. Are there ways in which you could better "model" the healing power of peace? Do you speak for peace in your church, community, and social circle? Do you reject violence— verbal and physical—in your family and among friends and colleagues? Do you choose the more difficult path of forgiveness rather than the easy way of grudges and revenge?

SATURDAY ▩ *Pray:* Father, Son, Spirit, please forgive us for the myriad ways in which we thwart your hope and the many opportunities you provide for universal peace and wellness. Help us to do better!

SEEKING GOD'S HEALING AT ALL COSTS

---

*They were trying to bring (the paralyzed man) in and lay him be-
fore Jesus; but finding no way...because of the crowd, they went up
on the roof and let him down...through the tiles...in front of Jesus.*
LUKE 5:18–19

What are we willing to endure to reach out to God and seek true healing?

Make no mistake: God does not put obstacles in our way when we truly seek him. The obstacles we encounter are human-made and sometimes of our own fashioning. There is the obstacle of our own voice telling us that God is too far away, too disinterested in our dis-ease to intervene with healing, so why bother asking. There is the obstacle of others telling us we must immediately pursue this treatment or that medicine or the other protocol because it may be our only hope. There is the clamor of fear, our own and that of others who may be affected by our unwellness. There is the secret conviction that we are not worthy to approach God for healing. There is the false sense of independence, when we tell ourselves we don't need God for every little problem. There is our lack of patience, our unwillingness to wait upon the Lord.

All of these are obstacles we must overcome so we can turn to God with a pure, seeking heart, desiring to be healed. The friends of the paralyzed man had no such obstacles when it came to seeking healing for him. They knew who was sitting in that crowded room, teaching, forgiving, and healing, and they knew they had to do anything in their power to bring their friend before him. They knew that it was folly to rely solely on themselves or others. If necessary, they would raise the roof. And that's precisely what they did.

SUNDAY ▪ *Pray:* Lord, help me to disassemble the "roof" of obstacles I've created between myself and your healing love.

MONDAY ▪ *Act:* Identify the obstacles that routinely keep you from turning sincerely to God for healing. List each on a separate piece of paper. Read each one aloud and then say, "I reject this obstacle," before crumpling the page and throwing it away. Make a strong effort to keep your life free of the obstacles you reject.

TUESDAY ▪ *Pray:* Jesus, help me to recognize your sincere love for me so that I may approach you without fear.

WEDNESDAY ▪ *Act:* Darken a room by pulling the blinds, shades, or curtains. Consider the obstacle that most hampers you from seeking God's healing. Think about how that obstacle thrives in the darkness; adjust the window coverings to let in a little light. Think about how that obstacle came into your life; let in more light. Think about everything that this obstacle prevents you from doing and enjoying. Let in all the light. And release the power of that obstacle.

THURSDAY ▪ *Pray:* Great Teacher, let me learn the lesson of humility so that I may stop relying on myself and turn wholeheartedly to you.

FRIDAY ▪ *Act:* Share this gospel passage with someone who is struggling with an obstacle that is keeping him or her from seeking God's healing.

SATURDAY ▪ *Pray:* Lord, gently remove anything that keeps me from seeking you.

Week Forty

HEALING WATERS OF SALVATION

With joy you will draw waters from the well of salvation. And you will say in that day: Give thanks to the LORD; call on his name; make known his deeds among the nations; proclaim that his name is exalted. ISAIAH 12:3–4

W ater was a huge deal in the desert that is much of the Middle East. Was and is. So it's not surprising that Scripture passages devoted to God's healing and forgiveness reference water. Bible academics may call it a motif, but in reality, water had—and has—many real and practical applications in Scripture and in life. Water was scarce and precious, and those with access to it were much more likely to live healthy, peaceful, and relatively long lives. Water was, literally, a substance of salvation for the body and soul; water was a gift from God, and Isaiah urges us to praise God's goodness in providing water.

Today, as then, water heals and saves. It seems that for any ailment, from a cold to an infection, the first bit of advice is: drink water, stay hydrated. And we know from celebrities and nonprofit organizations advocating for third world nations that the lack of clean water is potentially fatal.

The fact that water is an important part of our worship, from baptism forward, reflects water's life-giving, healing properties and elevates it to a substance of spiritual salvation as well. Isaiah was well aware of the role water had played in the salvation and healing of the Jews, from the parting of the Red Sea to God's provision of water through Moses to the Israelites in the desert. In the same way, we are aware of Jesus' use of water, from walking on the waves of the Sea of Galilee to making mud with his own saliva to cure a blind man. Water, like salvation, should not be taken for granted, and we must praise God for both, always.

SUNDAY ■ *Pray:* Lord, thank you for the amazing images of water in Scripture that remind me of its role in life, health, and salvation.

MONDAY ■ *Act:* Drink water! Be conscious of making the effort to drink enough water. To increase the healing prospects of water, substitute it for sugary drinks, coffee, or even juice to save calories and cleanse your system.

TUESDAY ■ *Pray:* Bountiful God, I praise you for providing water for day-to-day living and ask you to remind me of the importance of conservation and wise use.

WEDNESDAY ■ *Act:* When you bathe, clean, cook, brush your teeth, wash your hands, water plants—whenever you use water today—be conscious of your use. Acknowledge how important water is in your daily life and routine. Remember the many people worldwide who don't have enough water. Avoid waste and give God thanks for every drop that you have and use.

THURSDAY ■ *Pray:* Lord, forgive me for the times that I take for granted the many resources you provide, including water.

FRIDAY ■ *Act:* Research and donate to an organization that works to preserve water, to use water for energy purposes, or to bring water to regions of the world where people suffer because there isn't enough.

SATURDAY ■ *Pray:* Father, as your generosity flows through my life, let me "pay forward" your gifts to my greatest ability.

HEALING BEATITUDES

Then he looked up at his disciples and said: "Blessed are you who are poor, for yours is the kingdom of God. Blessed are you who are hungry now, for you will be filled. Blessed are you who weep now, for you will laugh." LUKE 6:20–21

A close reading of the gospels reveals that Jesus' teachings were not always a bowl of cherries. He asks much of us, as he did of the apostles. Yet there are few passages as comforting as these, traditionally called the Beatitudes, or the Blessings, that Jesus offers the crowd. Why comforting?

Because we are that crowd.

We have all been poor, if not financially, then in spirit; we have all hungered, if not for food, then for love, friendship, companionship, healing; we have all wept with sadness or joy, in illness, despair, and anger. To know that Jesus was speaking to us, offering each and every one of us these healing and comforting blessings, is a balm in and of itself.

But the Beatitudes are greater even than that. They are not just personal; they are universal. Every person in the world has experienced the conditions that Jesus describes: poverty, hunger, sorrow. There were thousands of people hearing these words, and those thousands represented the entire world; every class and type and age of person was present to hear this open-air teaching. And just as no one is excluded from the life experiences of poverty, hunger, and sorrow, so no one is excluded from Jesus' corresponding blessings or his promises of what is to come.

SUNDAY ▪ *Pray:* Jesus, remind me that when I feel most degraded in body, soul, mind, and spirit, that is when I am most blessed by you.

MONDAY ▪ *Act:* What are you hungry for? Is your stomach hungry for food? Is your mind hungry for a good book, challenging puzzle, or conversation? Is your body hungry for healing? Is your soul hungry for peace? Be conscious of the small and large ways that God offers to fill these needs for you today.

TUESDAY ▪ *Pray:* Lord, whenever I hunger, whatever I think I hunger for, fill me first with your presence.

WEDNESDAY ▪ *Act:* In what ways do you feel poor? Are you in financial trouble? Is there something you want that you probably can't afford? Does your body feel poorly? Is your brain sluggish? Is your spirit diminished? Be aware that these "impoverishments" may be ways that God is leading you to his kingdom.

THURSDAY ▪ *Pray:* Penniless Jesus, when I resent my lack of monetary wealth, teach me to rejoice in the poverty that brings me closer to you.

FRIDAY ▪ *Act:* Why do you feel like weeping? Are you mourning a loved one or a lost friendship? Do you feel betrayed? Are you sick and exhausted? Have you disappointed another? Or yourself? Go ahead and weep, knowing that God will provide you a time for laughter so resounding that it will blot out even the memory of tears.

SATURDAY ▪ *Pray:* Lord, when I feel like weeping, remind me that this life is passing, and only in you can all things become reasons for joy.

REFUGE FOR THE NEEDY AND POOR

O LORD, you are my God; I will exalt you, I will praise your name. For you have been a refuge to the poor, a refuge to the needy in their distress, a shelter from the rainstorm and a shade from the heat. ISAIAH 25:1, 4

T he people hit hardest by illness, dis-ease, depression, and oppression are often those least able to care for themselves or negotiate the health care system. These problems impact the very poor and disenfranchised most deeply. Indeed, one of the leading causes of bankruptcy in this country is the cost of health care. In other, poorer, countries with few or no public services and health care, the poor can be devastated by illness; a simple infection can be fatal.

These are not people who ask God for help after they phone their doctor, pick up their prescription, or check in with their insurer. When their children are sick or hurt, they don't stop off at church to pray for healing after a visit to the pediatrician, the allergist, the physical therapist. God is all they have: first, last, always. Isaiah knows this very well, and it is the cry of the poor and oppressed that he raises in his own cry in the passage above.

And it is a cry of praise! Despite their suffering, those most in need of healing recognize God not as a last resort but as a first and only resort. They bless and exalt him for this. I have a good friend who is unable to afford the best health care for her very ill parent. She is facing unimaginable (at least to me) challenges in addition to her parent's care. But when I try to sympathize with her, when I complain and rage about the unfairness of her situation, she simply says, "I can endure it all because I have God." And then she proceeds to do every impossibly difficult thing she has to do to get through every impossibly difficult day.

SUNDAY ■ *Pray:* Great God, I praise and thank you for absorbing all the pain and anguish in the world and for being with those who suffer and are afraid.

MONDAY ■ *Act:* Imagine what it would be like if you became sick and couldn't afford a doctor, had no insurance, didn't have access to or money for medicine/treatment, couldn't negotiate the health care system, and didn't know what to do. You only have God. How does this make you feel? How would you come to terms with this situation?

TUESDAY ■ *Pray:* Jesus, you showed me, in the breaking of your own body under the lash and on the cross, that you would always understand what it means for me to suffer pain. Thank you, Lord!

WEDNESDAY ■ *Act:* Pray for people in your community, state, country, and all over the world who have limited or no access to health care or medical treatment. Praise God, as Isaiah does, for being their refuge and resource.

THURSDAY ■ *Pray:* Lord, I seek the peace that comes with trusting you utterly, regardless of my state of mind or body. Help me, Lord!

FRIDAY ■ *Act:* Offer to volunteer at a clinic, hospital, convalescent home, or medical services program that helps the very poor.

SATURDAY ■ *Pray:* Father, give us the will to share your resources and show us how.

THE ULTIMATE HEALING

And Jesus said, "Young man, I say to you, rise!" The dead man sat up and began to speak, and Jesus gave him to his mother.
LUKE 7:14–15

This raising from the dead, which appears to have happened long before Jesus raised his friend Lazarus, gets surprisingly little attention. Chronologically in the Gospel of Luke, it occurs even before the more well-known raising of the young daughter of a wealthy man. In contrast with the Lazarus raising and that of the small girl, we have only a few lines to describe this encounter between Jesus and the widowed mother accompanying her son's funeral procession on the road from the village of Nain. While much of Israel almost instantly learned about the other two later raisings—and, indeed, it is believed that by raising Lazarus so publicly, Jesus sealed his own death warrant—this seems to be a more private, deeply personal experience focusing on Jesus and the mother and son. It is the story of Jesus showing compassion to an average, grieving woman: no one special, unknown to the Jewish nation, of no real consequence. This encounter feels off the grid, not on the agenda.

And for her and her son, Jesus is moved to perform the ultimate healing: he raises the young man from the dead.

This woman and her son could be any of us, and we can take great consolation in believing that the compassion demonstrated by Jesus toward them will be shown toward us. At that time, Jesus will take us beyond all illness, pain, sorrow. And like the young man, the first sight we see when he raises us will be his beautiful, glorious face.

SUNDAY ▧ *Pray:* Jesus, I thank you for the kindness you showed people when you lived among us, for it comforts me now.

MONDAY ▧ *Act:* Think about the last funeral or wake you attended. Imagine that Jesus, still not well-known or established, walked into the room, saw the devastated family, and compassionately raised the deceased from the casket. How would you feel? What would you do? What impact to you think it would have on those present?

TUESDAY ▧ *Pray:* Jesus, your compassion was so overwhelming that it flowed from you like a river; let me show even a trickle of such kindness.

WEDNESDAY ▧ *Act:* Imagine that you were not present at the raising described for Monday, but simply read an account of it in the newspaper. Do you think it would have made the front page? Would the article have a mocking tone? Would you respond with cynicism? Curiosity? Hope? Would you try to find or hear this Jesus?

THURSDAY ▧ *Pray:* Lord, when I feel cynical and doubtful, flood me with the brilliant illumination of knowing you.

FRIDAY ▧ *Act:* Spend time with someone who is grieving. Let the bereaved lead the conversation: if she or he wants to speak of the lost one, join in; if she or he wants to speak of other matters, go along; if she or he just wants to sit in silence, do so in as supportive and compassionate a way as you can.

SATURDAY ▧ *Pray:* Merciful God, let me someday hear you say, "My child, I say to you, rise!"

LORD, HELP MY UNBELIEF!

The boy...fell on the ground and rolled about, foaming at the mouth. Jesus asked the father, "How long has this been happening...?" He said, "From childhood...but if you are able to do anything, have pity on us and help us." Jesus said to him, "If you are able!—All things can be done for the one who believes." Immediately the father...cried out, "I believe; help my unbelief!"
MARK 9:20–24.

Jesus is frustrated! The father brought his child to Jesus' disciples, and they failed to heal him. Jesus has already rebuked them and the crowd for lack of faith. When the father also expresses doubt, Jesus reacts the way we all sometimes feel: he's had it with everyone! But when the father pathetically cries out "I believe; help my unbelief!" Jesus' compassion surges forth, and he heals the boy.

Was Jesus thinking about his own human parents, what they had endured for him, and all that Mary would yet suffer? Was Jesus' compassion an acknowledgment of the fearful love parents have for a hurting child?

Perhaps Jesus understood the father's faith in bringing the child to him. Risking humiliation and rejection, he'd taken a very sick boy with embarrassing, violent symptoms into a public place to seek healing. When the disciples' faith failed, the father's did not; he appealed directly to Jesus. Even after the father briefly wavered, provoking Jesus, the Lord pitied this man who had already demonstrated such faith.

This is one of the gospels' most heartening healings. We learn that Jesus was indeed human, subject to exasperation and anger, in this example of how completely he came to understand our physical and emotional frailties. Just as notable, we discover that God does not require perfect faith from us; Jesus is moved by the father's effort. God loves us, understands us, and wants our effort, honesty, and willingness to acknowledge his power...and our own weakness.

SUNDAY ▪ *Pray:* O my dear Lord, I do believe that you can heal me and do all things for me! Lord, I am only human! Please, Lord, help my unbelief!

MONDAY ▪ *Act:* Send a gift certificate to a parent you know who is struggling with a sick or troubled child. Enclose a note of encouragement and an offer to listen.

TUESDAY ▪ *Pray:* Jesus, strengthen my faith when it is too weak for me to even turn my face to you for healing. Have compassion on my humanity, Lord!

WEDNESDAY ▪ *Act:* Make a donation to a charity that helps impoverished, hungry, or sick children. With your donation enclose a note of thanks to the staff for their work and for giving you the opportunity to support it.

THURSDAY ▪ *Pray:* Lord, help me to accept your healing touch unquestioningly, as a child accepts medicine and healing ministrations from a beloved parent.

FRIDAY ▪ *Act:* If your church offers a ministry to help families and children, join it. If it doesn't, start one or join a related ministry. These programs can be as simple as collecting new winter coats and gloves for children, or as involved as "adopting" needy families.

SATURDAY ▪ *Pray:* Jesus, please heal the troubled and sick children in my life; help me to demonstrate my faith to them in whatever ways are most useful.

STRENGTH IN WEAKNESS

Strengthen the weak hands, and make firm the feeble knees. Say to those who are of a fearful heart, "Be strong, do not fear! Here is your God." ISAIAH 35:3–4

T here are times when we just can't seem to summon the courage to face God. We are beset with doubts, dismayed with ourselves, sick and tired of the world and our part in it. Isaiah is writing at a time in history when the Israelites were in precisely that position. They had been dis-eased and suffering for a long time. They did not dare turn their sin-stained, feverish faces to God and weren't sure they could if they wanted to. They had turned from God and made themselves sick with idolatry, division, and war.

Sound familiar?

America has become a nation glutted, yet not satisfied, with the idolatries of finance, fame, and food. Our leaders, perhaps reflecting our own angry divisions, are viciously partisan. Clutching our guns, we war among ourselves and solve global challenges with military force, while those who most stridently and self-righteously claim God do so seemingly to benefit their own agendas.

How do we, so sickened and in need of healing, find the bravery, individually or collectively, to turn to God?

Alone, we cannot. Collectively, we cannot. Without God's grace, we— like the Israelites of Isaiah's time—are too weak. But with God's grace, our weakness is transformed into his strength. God's strength makes use of our weakness to change our hearts and minds, souls and communities. And here's the good news: God's grace is ours for the asking. Be strong, do not fear! Here is your God.

SUNDAY ▓ *Pray:* Awesome Father, forgive me when, in my human weakness, I offend you, and school me in the power of your grace.

MONDAY ▓ *Act:* Do you "fear the Lord"? In what ways? List the ways—and reasons—you fear the Lord. Write with your "weak" hands, and then fall to your "feeble" knees and offer your fears to God, asking him to use his strength to erase your weakness and turn your fear to awe.

TUESDAY ▓ *Pray:* Jesus, when I am trembling in body and spirit, remind me that it was when your human body and spirit were at their weakest that your divine strength saved the world.

WEDNESDAY ▓ *Act:* Define God's grace. How does it work in your life, on your life? Do you believe that God's grace is accessible to you? How can God's gift of grace help you right now? Make an effort to feel, know, and live God's grace in at least one aspect of your life today.

THURSDAY ▓ *Pray:* Almighty God, when I would flee from the shadow of your power in shame and fear, show me the strength of your healing love.

FRIDAY ▓ *Act:* Invite God to work through you to show his strength to a weakened person in need of help. Boost his or her tentative faith by reading the letters of Saint Paul together. Explain how God's strength has made use of your own weakness. Share a meal or a coffee and listen. Pray together.

SATURDAY ▓ *Pray:* My Lord! Rescue me from the weakness and sickness and division of this world! Be my refuge, Lord!

MARCHING ORDERS

Then Jesus called the twelve together and gave them power and authority...and sent them out to proclaim the kingdom of God and to heal. LUKE 9:1–2

I t is worth noting that when Jesus sent the apostles out into the world, it was not just to proclaim the kingdom of God, as he had taught them; and it was not just to heal, as he had demonstrated for them. It was to do both—at the same time, in the same villages, among the same families, tribes, and nation.

Healing and the kingdom of God are deeply intertwined, if not the same thing. Where is healing perfected? Where are we elevated beyond the reach of human ills and anguish? In God's kingdom. By proclaiming the kingdom of God, the apostles were indeed announcing the time of perfect healing and wholeness. They were bringing God's kingdom to the world through both their and Jesus' teaching, and their and Jesus' healings.

Can we bring the kingdom of God in our world? Only if we ourselves are ready to receive the message. Observe that Jesus goes on to instruct the apostles to leave behind those towns and villages where their message is not welcome. The places and people who reject the Good News and its attendant physical and spiritual healing have actually rejected themselves as participants in the kingdom.

We, of course, do not think of ourselves as among those who would reject the word of God or the healing of God. How foolish would that be? But do we live out our opinions of ourselves? Are we agents of the word of God? Are we agents of God's healing both for ourselves and others? Are we prepared to be healed? Are we prepared for the kingdom of God?

SUNDAY ▧ *Pray:* Jesus, prepare me to receive your word: the kingdom of God and the perfect healing of my body, mind, and soul.

MONDAY ▧ *Act:* Consider one opportunity you've recently had—and lost—to bring the kingdom of God to another. How did you lose this opportunity? Why did you pass it up? Were you preoccupied? Out of patience? In a bad mood? Afraid to be rejected or embarrassed?

TUESDAY ▧ *Pray:* Lord, help me to discern your magnificence in every aspect of my life.

WEDNESDAY ▧ *Act:* Find or make an opportunity today to bring someone the good news of the kingdom of God. Use the lessons you learned about yourself on Monday to prepare to take advantage of any situation in which you might speak of—or show someone a little of—God's kingdom right here on earth.

THURSDAY ▧ *Pray:* Jesus, give me the knowledge and courage to be one of your evangelizing apostles in my world.

FRIDAY ▧ *Act:* Prepare yourself for the kingdom of God and its healing. During meditation, focus on emptying yourself of doubt and cynicism. Ask God to cleanse you of any thoughts or feelings that stand in the way of you fully experiencing the apostolic message. Breathe deeply, inviting God's spirit to be in you.

SATURDAY ▧ *Pray:* Jesus, help me to live your word and your healing in every thought, word, and action of my life.

AGELESS HEALER

The days are surely coming, says the LORD, when I will raise up for David a righteous Branch, and...in his days Judah will be saved and Israel will live in safety...He will be called, "The LORD is our righteousness." **JEREMIAH 23:5–6**

The entire Old Testament can be read as a witness to God as judge sometimes but as healer always, throughout every age of humankind. For as often as people have turned away from his healing and righteousness, he has remained ready to take them back. As often as we have sinned, God has offered forgiveness.

The Jews are living through such a time during Jeremiah's prophetic days. Having rejected God and chosen corruption and idolatry, they are in desperate straits, losing wars and being taken captive. Their economy and coherence as a people are being destroyed. Jeremiah is known as the prophet of woe, constantly telling the Jews what they most don't want to hear and being consistently persecuted for it.

But here, he becomes a messianic prophet. Not only will God restore his people, Jeremiah is saying, but God will send the messiah, so good and so strong that he will be called the Lord is our righteousness, to save the people.

We know this messiah to be Jesus, and we know that God chose to send him to us—this amazing, righteous one, this Son of God—as a human being! Not to judge us sternly, for when Jesus comes, he experiences all that we humans experience, and his compassion and love temper his judgment.

Which is a very good thing for the rest of us.

SUNDAY *Pray:* Lord, I praise you for coming to us in gentleness and kindness, to teach us how we should live as men and women.

MONDAY *Act:* Read the books of Jeremiah and Isaiah, taking special note of the messianic prophecies. How do you respond to this call of readiness? In what ways do you prepare to welcome the messiah, the lord of healing, into your life? In what ways do you need to be healed?

TUESDAY *Pray:* Father, when I fear that I can't be healed or forgiven, remind me that you can do all these things…and more.

WEDNESDAY *Act:* Make a list of anything—any pain, humiliation, sorrow, irritation, temptation—that you have suffered but that Jesus did not suffer. Hang the blank sheet somewhere visible so that you can be reminded of what kind of God is your God.

THURSDAY *Pray:* Lord, cleanse me of self-pity so that I may lift my face to you and shoulder those burdens you have given me.

FRIDAY *Act:* Define righteousness. What did God mean when, through Jeremiah and others, he called his messiah "righteous"? How was Jesus righteous? How is healing a righteous act? How can you become more righteous, more healed, more of a healer?

SATURDAY *Pray:* Jesus, thank you for being a righteous messiah and man, and help me to become more righteous by following you.

FAULTLESS HEALING

The disciples asked him, "Rabbi, who sinned, this man or his parents, that he was born blind?" Jesus answered, "Neither...; he was born blind so that God's works might be revealed in him."
JOHN 9:2–3

I n the days of Jesus, calamity or visible illness was thought to be visited upon individuals as a result of sin—if not theirs, then that of their parents. The worse the illness or tragedy, the greater the assumed sin. So the disciples automatically assume that a man born blind had to be carrying around a massive burden of sin, to the point that they judged him perhaps guilty of sin before he was punished for the sin by being born blind. Doesn't seem very logical, does it?

But is it so different today?

How often have we heard someone (perhaps ourselves?) wail, "What have I done to deserve this?" or "Things are so bad, God must be punishing me!"? More in line with the comments of the disciples, how often have we thought such things about some other sick or unfortunate person?

It can feel much easier to "blame the victim" than to acknowledge that suffering can befall anyone at any time without any humanly explicable reason. We don't like that kind of uncertainty because it means that we could be the next ones to suffer or fall ill. It's easier to think that there's a reason for another's suffering.

Oh, she fell and broke her ankle? Well, that's what she gets for wearing those ridiculous high heels.

Oh, he has skin cancer? Guess he's regretting all those days lazing at the beach now.

Jesus puts an end to such idle speculation. Only God knows the purpose of suffering, and only God knows what can be achieved through it.

SUNDAY ▪ *Pray:* Merciful Jesus, I praise you for modeling compassion and righteousness in an age of blame and guilt.

MONDAY ▪ *Act:* Repent of any assumptions you've made about why someone has suffered or become ill. If you were arrogant enough to have faulted the person to his or her face, sincerely apologize. If you faulted the person to others, let them know that you were wrong. Most importantly, ask God's forgiveness.

TUESDAY ▪ *Pray:* Rabbi, teach me to view all people with your keen, loving eyes.

WEDNESDAY ▪ *Act:* Consider someone who has seemingly "brought on" her or his own suffering or sickness, like a drinker with a liver ailment or a diabetic with a sweet tooth. Compassionately consider the origins of his or her problem. Is he physically addicted to alcohol? Is she overindulging because she has been hurt or rejected? Replace judgment with empathy.

THURSDAY ▪ *Pray:* Jesus, let my compassion and openheartedness for others—and for myself—know no limits.

FRIDAY ▪ *Act:* Do you now think or have you ever thought: "God is punishing me" because of an illness or challenge in your life? Why do, or did, you think that way? Is this how you were taught to think about misfortune? Do you feel guilty or superstitious? Ask God to help you transform such thinking into a prayer for help.

SATURDAY ▪ *Pray:* Lord, free me from bad, old ways of thinking and from crippling guilt.

JESUS/GOD, THE HOLY ONE: HEALER AND SAVIOR

―――――――――

Take courage, my children, cry to God, and he will deliver you...joy has come to me from the Holy One, because of the mercy that will soon come to you from your everlasting savior.
BARUCH 4:21, 22

Baruch, though perhaps not as well known, is another messianic prophet. Again, we see an enlivening cry to courage for the people of Israel, a people broken, wounded, and ill, unable to deliver themselves, heal themselves, or forgive themselves. Baruch's vision here is not of an avenging and powerful messiah but of a merciful savior, an everlasting savior, a savior of joy and deliverance.

When you stop to think about it, how could Jesus have been and meant so much to so many people in so many places? One man, with a few uninfluential followers, walking up and down the small country that is now Israel, and yet he transformed the world. The prophets of Israel expected him, his own people mostly rejected him, and afterward much of the world came to follow and hallow him. The diversity in the Christian world alone is enough to demonstrate Jesus as Savior.

But for all the prophetic predictions of Jesus, of all the messianic prophecies, Baruch's may be the most human. This is not a savior to fear, despite our sins and mistakes; this is not a savior to destroy, despite the evil in the world; this is not a savior to rule from afar with an iron rod, despite the need of humans for leadership. This is a savior to deliver us from sin and illness and enmity, to give us courage in a sick and divisive world, to bring us joy in the very thought of his presence, to be everlasting so as to never abandon us to ourselves, and, most of all, to show us the mercy we so deeply need and too often may not deserve or be capable of seeking except from God.

SUNDAY ■ *Pray:* Jesus, I give thanks that all the wondrous prophecies about you taken together still could not do justice to who you are.

MONDAY ■ *Act:* Imagine that you are hearing about Jesus for the first time, that you are reading or hearing a messianic prophecy of a savior about to come and change everything—for you, for your world, for the world. What would you feel? What might you think? Would you believe? Would you be excited? Afraid? What would you expect?

TUESDAY ■ *Pray:* Beloved Savior, please deliver me from my sins and sicknesses, and make me whole in you.

WEDNESDAY ■ *Act:* How do you define salvation? Is the definition different when you apply it to the world versus just yourself? What do you expect it to be like when Jesus returns? Do you think you know who will be "saved"? List the ways you want Jesus to "save" you.

THURSDAY ■ *Pray:* Jesus, let me always have an awareness of and access to the joy that comes in loving you.

FRIDAY ■ *Act:* Choose one of the ways from your Wednesday list that you want Jesus to "save" you and apply it to another person. If you want Jesus to save you by forgiving you, forgive another; if by giving you courage, encourage another; if by being your friend, befriend another; if by healing you, offer healing thoughts, prayers, or health-related assistance to another.

SATURDAY ■ *Pray:* Lord, I need your mercy every moment of every day; let me experience it, Lord, and be changed by it.

Week Fifty

HEALING BREAD OF LIFE

Jesus said to them, "I am the bread of life. Whoever comes to me will never be hungry, and whoever believes in me will never be thirsty. " JOHN 6:35

J esus frightened and offended some Jews with statements like this, including some of his followers, who, John later tells us, turned away after he offered them his flesh. They could not understand or accept this teaching. For many, it seemed too literal and distressing. But what does Jesus' declaration mean to us? Do we fully recognize the healing power of Christ as the bread of life?

Jesus was not only speaking about the Holy Eucharist, since he had not yet instituted it among his apostles at the time when he said these words to the Jews. He had, however, already made several references to himself as the living water for those who thirst, most notably to the outlier Samaritan woman. She was, in her own way, ostracized and in need of healing, and, in keeping with his ministry to the disenfranchised, it was to her that Jesus clearly offered the water of life.

In presenting himself to the Jews—and us—as the one to end our hunger and thirst, Jesus is doing nothing less than offering divine medicine for an ailing world and people. For all the other things that Jesus was, is, and will be, and in view of the essential sacrament of the Holy Eucharist, both the teachings of the Lord and his Body and Blood combine to provide the healing elixir of life across the ages. They nourish us, spiritually and physically. They provide us with peace and understanding. They comfort and console us.

Jesus wasn't trying to frighten or offend the Jews; he was trying to heal them. They simply couldn't see it. Can we?

SUNDAY ░ *Pray:* Jesus, I am not worthy to receive you! And yet you offer yourself despite my unworthiness, Lord! Words fail to describe your gift!

MONDAY ░ *Act:* Meditate on God's gift of the Holy Eucharist. Consider the healing, restorative, and merciful properties as you try to absorb the magnitude of this gift.

TUESDAY ░ *Pray:* Lord, I thank you for the healing properties of Holy Communion for my mind, body, and soul.

WEDNESDAY ░ *Act:* Today, or the next time it is possible, take Holy Communion. Prepare yourself first. Fast. Pray. Confess your sins and ask for forgiveness. Be conscious of the Body and Blood entering your body. Stay after Mass to offer thanks.

THURSDAY ░ *Pray:* Father, you allowed humankind to kill and consume your Son, our Savior, so that you could raise him and offer him to us as everlasting sustenance. Father, accept my inadequate praise and gratitude, for I know that if I spent my life in praise, it would not be enough.

FRIDAY ░ *Act:* Jesus established the Holy Eucharist in part to provide a unifying sacrament for all who would follow him. Promote this unity by offering to bring someone—or even a family—to church and Holy Communion with you. Consciously share the joy of Mass and the Holy Eucharist.

SATURDAY ░ *Pray:* Lord, I take comfort in knowing that you are nearer to me than I am to myself.

TRANSFORMATIVE RESTORATION

I will give them one heart, and put a new spirit within them; I will remove the heart of stone from their flesh and give them a heart of flesh. EZEKIEL 11:19

I t sometimes seems beyond our comprehension that God could be so patient, so merciful, so willing to wait us out in the face of our sin, stubbornness, dis-ease, and disobedience. In this prophecy from Ezekiel, God is not just saying that he will give each of his people, who have hardened their hearts against him, a new heart. It is much more than that. He will give them something better than the human hearts that have betrayed them in the past by allowing them to turn from him; God will give them something of his own creation: a heart of flesh. And not many individual hearts of flesh but one heart!

One unifying heart. One heart of flesh for all people. One heart that is turned toward God. And if it is turned toward God, the people who have it within them will be healed by God.

The transformative restoration described here in Ezekiel is breathtaking. It is God literally re-creating his people, giving them new life and renewed spirit from one source, giving them another chance to be healed and made one people under God.

Why is it so easy to harden our hearts against God? Humans have done it across the ages, from the time we were first aware of God. We do it out of fear, out of a need to feel independent, out of anger, out of resentment for our mortality, out of sickness.

But God is telling us here that we don't have to, that he is ready to do spiritual surgery on us and bring us back to what we are meant to be. Then, now, and always.

SUNDAY ▨ *Pray:* Lord, when my heart turns to stone within me because of anger, illness, or fear, restore it to "a heart of flesh," ready to accept you.

MONDAY ▨ *Act:* It is no surprise that a heart is about the size of a small fist; after all, are we not constantly closing our hearts in anger, frustration and dis-ease, as we do our fists? Today, be conscious of keeping your fists open into hands willing to give and receive generously and with God's transforming love.

TUESDAY ▨ *Pray:* Father, it seems that every day I am in need of restorative transformation! Have mercy on me and bring me closer to you with each "change of heart."

WEDNESDAY ▨ *Act:* Find a rock about the size of a fist and put it where you will frequently see it to help you guard against letting your heart become a heavy stone.

THURSDAY ▨ *Pray:* Lord, cleanse me of the stubbornness that makes me return to my old ways, so that I may learn and live your ways.

FRIDAY ▨ *Act:* You would never consciously turn a heart of stone toward God. But what about toward others? Remembering that the heart you show others is the heart seen by God, make an effort to deliberately open your heart toward someone against whom you have closed it in the past.

SATURDAY ▨ *Pray:* Patient, Beloved God, I rejoice in your willingness to restore and heal me again and again and again.

SO SIMPLE

Jesus answered (Nicodemus): "For God so loved the world that he gave his only Son, so that everyone who believes in him may not perish but may have eternal life." JOHN 3:10, 16

I s it really that simple?

Could it really be true that all we have to do is accept God's love by accepting the gift that Jesus was and is, and by believing in him, God's only Son?

Well, yes, it is that simple. But it's not necessarily that easy.

Nicodemus, a great scholar and teacher of God's law, had a difficult time grasping Jesus' meaning, because, what does it mean, really, to believe in him?

Is it just a matter of words? "I believe in Jesus"...and everything becomes perfect, all is well, we are healed and have everlasting life?

I think there is more to it. I think believing in Jesus, in God, in the healing power of the Holy Spirit requires more, something deeper, a wordless affirmation, a faith that may tremble in the face of malaise and tragedy but that nevertheless holds to God.

When I first started writing about my experience with cancer, I received a note from an older woman who had been living with cancer. We started a correspondence. Physically, her situation was much worse than mine. But she had an extraordinary depth of faith. One day, after she'd been through some tests, I shot her an e-mail: "How are you?" Soon, I received her reply, made in the context of this great faith: "Today, I have a feeling of well-being."

Not: "I am in remission." Not: "I am pain free." Not: "The new treatment is working." But: "I have a feeling of well-being."

This is the level of faith, of preparedness, I seek.

Simple, but not easy.